# FLUFFY

a play in two acts by

David Overton

# Uproar Theatrics

**LICENSING & PRODUCTION INQUIRIES**
**Uproar Theatrics, LLC.**
**hello@uproartheatrics.com I www.UproarTheatrics.com**

*Fluffy* copyright © 2021 by David Overton

*Fluffy* is published by Uproar Theatrics, LLC
500 8th Ave FRNT 3, #1714 New York, NY 10018

ISBN: 978-1-968051-07-5

First Printing, May 2025

FLUFFY

## CAST OF CHARACTERS
FLUFFY: Male. Teens to 20s. Flamboyant, slinky, no-nonsense, beautiful cat.
DELILAH: Female. 20s to 30s. Intellectual, attractive, poised, singer.
PEPE: Male. 20s to 30s. Dashing, confident, energetic, gay, Latino, singer, plays guitar, bilingual (Spanish and English).
NANCY: Female. 40s to 50s. Delilah's mother. Traditional, provincial, opinionated, singer.
CARMELITA: Female. Teens to 20s. Sexy, saucy, Latina, bilingual (Spanish and English) cat.

## SETTING
All of the action takes place in Delilah's apartment. A second scene is added in Act II to denote the passing of time.

## MUSIC
There are two instances of live music in Fluffy. The first is Pepe accompanying himself on guitar singing "Poesia" or another Spanish-style lullaby (for which you have acquired all rights and permissions for use in performance). Please see the appendix for the sheet music. For learning purposes, a link to a recording of "Poesia," can be found on the show page at Uproar Theatrics under the instrumentation section.

The second use of music is during the wedding: Delilah and Nancy sing Schubert's "Ave Maria" in the background. The sheet music is readily available as part of the public domain. Arrange/accompany as best suits your production.

PLAYWRIGHT'S NOTES:
FLUFFY celebrates acceptance, resilience, and diversity. All of the characters were written with love, humor, and respect. One of the most appealing aspects to owning a cat is simply watching them move. Their slinkiness, agility, flexibility, and fluidity in motion can be mesmerizing; therefore, the actors playing FLUFFY and CARMELITA should be excellent movers.

FLUFFY often speaks directly to the audience. When FLUFFY speaks to other characters onstage, it's almost as if the other characters fully understand what FLUFFY is saying, but mostly it's an unusually accurate understanding of what the cat is communicating to the human.

CARMELITA oftentimes speaks in Spanish. For reference, I have provided English translations after some of her lines in brackets. However, the actress playing CARMELITA should use the Spanish dialogue in performance.

"A cat is the delight of a household. All day long a comedy is played out by an incomparable actor." – Champfleury (a.k.a., Jules François Felix Fleury-Husson, 1821 – 1889)

*Original cat artwork by Riley Shea Overton

FLUFFY

ACT I

Scene 1

SETTING: *It is Saturday, eight o'clock on a spring morning, in the living room of* DELILAH; *a single, middle-aged woman who lives in a studio apartment, alone, with lots of books and her cat,* FLUFFY. *There is a couch with fabric covering, some bookcases, a chair-and-a-half, an area rug, a sturdy coffee table just in front of the couch, and a small dining table with two chairs near a small kitchenette. A very large window on the back wall shows a beautiful view of a large, American city. Below the window is a narrow table with picture frames and a vase with flowers. Other attractive art decorations are on the walls. There are two doors: one that opens to the bedroom/bathroom and one that is the main entry door. There is also a three- to four-foot-tall scratching post by the dining table.* FLUFFY *wears a handsome collar with a large 'diamond' and is turned upstage sitting in what would be a "crisscross, applesauce" position except that he has one leg extended to the side. He is grooming himself, as cats do. For much of the play,* FLUFFY *speaks directly to the audience.*

FLUFFY

(*looks over his shoulder to audience; then, dryly*) Meow. (*turns back upstage, continues grooming himself for a few moments, then looks over his shoulder again*) I'm trying to get something here. I'll be with y'all in a minute. (*continues*

## FLUFFY (CONT)

*grooming himself for a few moments then whips around in a flash and smiles at the audience for an extended beat.*)
Hello. (*not angrily, but with a winning smile*) I said, 'hello.' Yes, 'hello' to you! And you! And especially you! Before we start, I just want to say 'thank you all' for coming out to see me. Y'all gonna enjoy seeing me. I mean, that's why y'all came, right? Oh, I know there's other people gonna be up here, but I'm the focus. After all, my name is Fluffy. Yeah, I know. What's up with the name 'Fluffy'? They didn't put much thought into it. In fact, seems like they didn't put any thought into it. Look at me. I ain't fluffy. I'm smooth. Real smooth. Like butter. Like Etta James. Like Barbara Streisand's voice. Now, some of y'all don't know who Etta James and Barbara Streisand are but trust me, their voices? They smooth. Like butter. Like me. But my human named me Fluffy and so I live with it. Now, as a cat, we have our own names but they're too hard for people to pronounce so we go with what we are given by our pets – I mean, our humans – but when we are with other cats? We use our real names. I know some of y'all out there are thinking, 'I bet I could pronounce it.' Uh-uh. You couldn't. And what's more, you wouldn't accept it. You'd think, 'Why did he name himself that?' Or, 'What kind of name is that?' See, if it ain't comfortable for you; if it's not something you used to, then you dismiss it. But, since I can see in your eyes that you really want to know my name, I'll tell you. (*clears his throat, let's out a long sexy, nasty, but mellifluous 'meow' then glances around the audience for any sign of understanding. Then, after a moment.*) See? Told you. So, y'all can just call me 'Fluffy.' Now, I know there are – how shall I say? Other 'entertainments' about creatures like me. Cats? They sing. They dance. There's a whole lot of them doing all sorts of things. Ridiculous, right? Well, it is. They're working too hard! I mean, look at them. They're running. And leaping. And sweating. No cat that I know does that. In fact, we do as little as possible. That's the way it works. You know what

FLUFFY (CONT)

I'm talking about. Consider this, when someone asks, 'what would you do for a million dollars?' the only answer that a forward thinking, enlightened being should respond with is, 'as little as possible.' That's what a smart creature says. That's what a cat says. That's what I say.

> DELILAH *enters wearing workout clothes and carrying a yoga mat.*

FLUFFY

Oh, here she comes! Here she comes! (*excitedly begins walking around her on two legs, rubbing himself against her, purring, then goes onto hands and knees and rubs against her legs*) This is the best part of the day! Meow! Meeeeoooowww!! Meeeeoooooooooooow!!!

DELILAH

Oh, Fluffy! Who's the good boy? Who's the good boy?

FLUFFY

I've been up all night and I'm so hungry! Meow! Meow!

DELILAH

Do you want breakfast? Is that what you want? Breakfast?

FLUFFY

Meooooowww!

> DELILAH *goes to the refrigerator, takes out an already-opened can of cat food that has either foil or a 'cat food cover' on it, scoops out a chunk of food and plops it into the cat bowl on the floor.* FLUFFY *has been following her around and rubbing on her while she does this.*

FLUFFY *goes over to bowl, sniffs at the food a few times, then turns to audience.*

## FLUFFY
(*to audience*) Meow. It's cold. I don't like it when it's cold. (*whistles*) Hey! Delilah? It's cold.

## DELILAH
What's wrong?

## FLUFFY
It's cold.

## DELILAH
It's what?

## FLUFFY
Cold. It's cold!

## DELILAH
(*assumes* FLUFFY *is miffed because the food is cold*) I know it's cold but that is what you get.

## FLUFFY
Do I look like a fool?

## DELILAH
Oh, baby (*scratching him under his chin*).

## FLUFFY
Did I do something wrong?

## DELILAH
What is it? You want your food? It's over there.

4

FLUFFY

(*looks over at the food*) That? Yeah, I know the food's over there. But are you serious?

DELILAH

Go eat it!

FLUFFY

I don't believe this.

DELILAH

(*grabbing* FLUFFY *around the middle as if she's picking him up*) Come on, baby.

FLUFFY

Whoa! Whooooaa! Meooooww!

DELILAH

There you go.

FLUFFY

Well. If I must. (*eats*)

*Meanwhile,* DELILAH *places her yoga mat in the middle of the room, sits in half-lotus on the mat, takes a deep breath, and closes her eyes.*

FLUFFY

(*licking his lips*) That. Was amazing. Temperature notwithstanding, but that was mighty fine! That's like a fish-blend pâté. Honestly, I don't even want to know what kind of fish that was, but that's the only way to start the day. (*to* DELILAH, *then "more"*) Meow. Meow? Meooowww!!

DELILAH

Did you like that? Huh? Did you?

FLUFFY

("*yes*") Meow.


DELILAH

What a prima donna. So picky.


FLUFFY

Meow! Picky? Honestly?


DELILAH

My baby. (*she gives him a nuzzle then resumes her meditation*)


FLUFFY

Aw, that's nice. That's Delilah. And what she's doing? She calls that 'yoga.' Supposed to be healthy. A mind and body experience. People are so funny. They don't know how to be healthy. Me? I'm just healthy in my daily way of being. I stretch every day. I practice personal hygiene every day. I eat fish every day. Well, almost every day. She gives me other sorts of food that I could swear has cheese and some sort of meat in it. I don't know what it is. Tastes like chicken. (*goes over to* DELILAH *and tries to sit in her lap*)


DELILAH

Not now, Fluffy. Not now.


FLUFFY

Meow! Come on, rub me, pet me, scratch me! Meow!


DELILAH

I can't right now. Look, you can sit beside me. I am trying to focus.

FLUFFY

Meow! All right. If that's the way it is. I'll just let you be.
I'm gonna go chill up on my spot. (*He sashays to the table
under the window, hops up and stretches out.*) What a view.
And let me tell you something, when the sun hits this area?
Heaven. (*beat*) And – what is that? Is that? Airplane? A bird.
That's a bird. Hey! Delilah! Meooow?! There's a bird out
there! Delilaaahh!

DELILAH

What is it?

FLUFFY

Meow! Meow! (DELILAH *resumes her meditation*)

DELILAH

Would you please stop being a crazy cat and calm down!

FLUFFY

I'm serious! Meow! (*beat*) All right, all right. Just be quiet.
Maybe it'll get close. Come on. A little closer. A little closer.
That's it. I'll kill that feathered fool! (*suddenly jumps up the
windowpane*) Meooww!! Oh, did you see that? Delilah! Did
you see that? So close!

DELILAH

What is it, Fluffy? What did you see? Did you see a bird? No
wonder you've got the zooms.

FLUFFY

("*yes*") Meooww!! Oh, Delilah! Did you see that bird? Did
you see how close I got? Oh, you would have been so proud
of me! I would've caught that bird, put it right at your feet,
you would have been so proud! This pane of glass was the
only thing protecting that bird! I would have gotten it! (*goes
to window and looks out*) Yeah! You keep on flying, fool! I'll

FLUFFY (CONT)

get you next time! You'd be so proud of me, you probably'd
want to get me some of that five dollar-a-can gourmet food!

DELILAH

Fluffy! That jump you did was murder! You could have
pulled a muscle. Or found enlightenment. Do you want a
treat? (*goes to get treats from basket on dining table*)

FLUFFY

Oh, yes! Meeeoow!!

DELILAH

Here's a treat. Eh, take two. (*goes back to her yoga, different
position*)

FLUFFY

Oh, you're too good to me. (*finishes eating the treats, looks
at* DELILAH *hopefully*) That is satisfaction. Unless you
want to give me another? Maybe? Meow?

DELILAH

You can't possibly want another.

FLUFFY

Yes, I could, actually possibly want another.

DELILAH

Let what you have digest. You know what happens if you eat
too much.

FLUFFY

If I eat too much? You gonna throw that in my face right
now? Fine. (*resumes his position by the window*) It's all clear
up here. By the window. No birds. In case you're wondering.

DELILAH'S *cell phone begins ringing.*

## DELILAH

What? Oh, give me strength. Mom. You can wait. (*cell phone stops ringing*)

## FLUFFY

She's going to call back. (*cell phone begins ringing again*) Meow.

## DELILAH

Fine. (*picks up*) Hello?

## NANCY

(*on speakerphone or projected onto a screen with sound*) Delilah?

## DELILAH

Yes, mother. You got me. How are you?

## NANCY

I just tried to call and you didn't pick up.

## DELILAH

Yes, I know. I was busy. (*moves into a different yoga position*)

## NANCY

Are you OK?

## DELILAH

I'm fine. Just stretching my body. And mind.

## NANCY

You're doing what?

## DELILAH

Yoga. I'm doing my yoga.

NANCY

I don't know why you do that. My friend Judy says that it's like some sort of voodoo.

DELILAH

Mother, like most physical activity, yoga has nothing to do with voodoo.

NANCY

But it does! Isn't it those 'certain' people or – or – whatever, atheists?

DELILAH

It's a wellness regime, a mindfulness practice. Many people do it and as far as I know, they're not atheists. (*beat*) Ma?

NANCY

Yes?

DELILAH

You called. What did you want to talk with me about?

NANCY

Oh, right, I just get confused when you start talking like that.

DELILAH

Talking like 'that', or talking at all?

NANCY

I – wait, what?

DELILAH

Nothing. Mother, speak…and I'll *not*.

NANCY

I just wanted to know if you could sing at a wedding. The couple asked for me but I don't think I'm going to be available, so I told them that you were my daughter and were just as good.

DELILAH

Singing at weddings has worn me thin, mother. Every time I go, Deacon Allen tracks me down and becomes condescending and annoying.

NANCY

Well, it's a wedding. He won't be there.

DELILAH

I suppose that's true. (*moves into a different yoga position*) Though he does have a propensity for appearing, unbidden, before me.

NANCY

Well, don't do it if you don't want to. I just thought you could use the money.

DELILAH

Oh, I could use the money. Who couldn't?

NANCY

Well, -

DELILAH

I'll take it, mother, I'll take it.

FLUFFY

Wait. You gonna sing at church again?

DELILAH

Is there anything else, ma, that requires conversation?

FLUFFY

You know what your gramma always used to say, "Singing in church is like praying twice!"

NANCY

I have some clothes that I got for you and I just wanted to make sure you were home and I'll drop them off. (*beat*) Hello? Will you be home?

DELILAH

I'll be home.

NANCY

You're not going out?

DELILAH

Not as of yet, no.

NANCY

I wish you'd get out more. You could meet someone.

FLUFFY

Oh! She doesn't need anyone!

NANCY

You know?

FLUFFY

She has me!

NANCY

Like a man?

FLUFFY

I'm the only man she needs!

12

DELILAH

Ah. Man. The being in servitude to his whims.

NANCY

In servitude to his what?

FLUFFY

His whims!

NANCY

His whims?

DELILAH

Mom, listen to me. I said I didn't have plans *yet*. I may go out, if I'm flagging in my resolve.

NANCY

You're flagging in your what?

DELILAH

I said I may go out.

NANCY

Oh, good, you could meet a man!

FLUFFY

Hey, we've been through this!

DELILAH

And I might not.

FLUFFY

Thank you!

NANCY

Delilah?

DELILAH

Might just stay home and revise an article for The New
Yorker.


NANCY

Oh, how boring! Go out! Have a good time!


DELILAH

And are you going out tonight?


NANCY

No, I have to see my chiropractor. My back and neck are
killing me.


DELILAH

How boring.


FLUFFY

(*laughs obnoxiously*) Ha, ha, ha!


NANCY

What?


DELILAH

Just wondering why our conversations can never pass the
Bechdel test.


NANCY

Who's Bechdel?


DELILAH

Never mind.


NANCY

Now, wait. I want to know who this Bechdel fellow is.

DELILAH

Bechdel is not a fellow, it's a woman – a woman's last name.
And if you're really interested in what the Bechdel test is,
look it up.

NANCY

I suppose, I could, when I –

DELILAH

Look, is there anything else, mommy dearest?

NANCY

No, I just wanted to make sure you were going to be in later.
I have some clothes that I got for you.

DELILAH

You told me as much.

NANCY

I told you about what?

DELILAH

About the clothes.

NANCY

Yeah, I have some clothes that I got for you.

DELILAH

I remember.

NANCY

OK, so, I'll see you later.

DELILAH

Yes, I remember that, too.

NANCY

Bye!

DELILAH

Bye (*looks at* FLUFFY *for a beat*).

FLUFFY

Meow.

DELILAH

What?!

FLUFFY

Are you familiar with Jean Paul-Sartre and his definition of Hades?

DELILAH

I see you. Looking at me. Don't you begin to philosophize with me.

FLUFFY

No fire and brimstone in Hades. Just other people who you can't get along with.

DELILAH

Why do you think I live alone?

FLUFFY

Honestly, I don't see how you put up with her.

DELILAH

You're judging me, aren't you?

FLUFFY

I'm a cat. So, meow.

DELILAH

What else am I going to do? She's my mother. (*tries a different yoga position*)

FLUFFY

I know that. Still. (*scrutinizes her yoga*) OK, that looks really uncomfortable. Why don't you try this (*goes into his own yoga pose, he's very good*). Or this (*another*). Or, how about this! (*a third*)

DELILAH

Show off. (*cell phone rings*) Again? (*picks up, on speakerphone, or projection as before*) Yes, mom?

NANCY

Forgot to ask, do you want me to put you on the schedule for next month?

DELILAH

Yes. Just not the 8 o'clock, please.

NANCY

The 8 o'clock's what's available!

DELILAH

It's just so early.

NANCY

Early? And, please. What are you doing at night that makes it impossible for you to get up the next morning by, what? Seven-fifteen?

DELILAH

Might be going out.

FLUFFY

No!

NANCY

You're going out?


DELILAH

No.


NANCY

I thought you said you were going out.


DELILAH

'Might.' I said I might be going out.


FLUFFY

Please, no!


NANCY

That's great! You might meet someone!


DELILAH

Nothing would make <u>you</u> happier.


NANCY

So, can I put you on the schedule for next month?


DELILAH

I've already said yes.


NANCY

OK, great, bye!


DELILAH

Bye.


FLUFFY

(*crossing himself, as a Catholic*) Oh, our Lady of 'I Can't
Even Today,' pray for us. Seriously, you are going to give me
a heart attack. I can't live like this.

#### DELILAH
What's the matter, Fluffy? You think I'm going to leave you?

#### FLUFFY
Meow.

#### DELILAH
Huh? You think I'm going to leave you?

#### FLUFFY
(*almost sobbing*) Yes. Meow. I do.

#### DELILAH
Oh, come now. Not even gone that long. (*starts to pick up* FLUFFY) Come on. Let's put you in your spot. (FLUFFY *immediately jumps down and looks at her*) Don't want to be up there? Suit yourself.

#### FLUFFY
I always do. (*beat*) Mostly, I just want to be near you.

#### DELILAH
All right, Fluffy, I'm going to take a quick shower. (FLUFFY *follows her around as she puts away yoga mat*) Oh! Fluffy, you are just under foot right now. (*trips over him*) Why are you following me around? Space, please. I guess you won't follow me into the shower, will you?

#### FLUFFY
(*quick, sharp*) Meeooww! I don't know how you do that shower thing!

#### DELILAH
What?

#### FLUFFY
Water!

DELILAH

Yes, I'm going to shower. Oh, and while I'm gone: the rug. Please do not destroy it any further.


FLUFFY

We'll see about that. Hey! Hey! Can I have a treat? Meow?


DELILAH

What? A treat?


FLUFFY

Meow!


DELILAH

OK. But you're going to get fat.


FLUFFY

I beg to differ, gimme the treat!


DELILAH

Oh, fine. (*gives another treat*)


FLUFFY

(*between chewing and crunching*) I would say thank you, but this is so good! Seriously, what do they put in this? Hey, wait! Before you go, could you at least leave something for me to entertain myself with? (*she goes*) Please?! (DELILAH *returns with a towel and puts it on the narrow table under the big window*) Oh, nice! (*goes up on the table, makes himself comfortable as* DELILAH *exits, sound of shower starts almost immediately*) This is good. This. Is. Good. (*to audience*) You could say I've got it made here. I get brushed. I get scratched. She lets me sit on her lap. She feeds me twice a day and she gives me as many treats as I can get out of her! But sometimes, the best part is when I know she's home – like now, in the shower – but she's not in sight. And

## FLUFFY (CONT)

when she's not in sight, I can make a more thorough inspection of things. Mmm-hmm. Mmm-hmm! This window needs cleaning. Just saying. And these flowers? Her mom sent them over because yesterday was her birthday. Now, if you'll excuse me for a moment, I would like to investigate. (*Tentatively, he begins touching his nose to the flowers and flicking his head to make the scent go away. He starts to chew on the leaves and flick his head.*) Mmmm. That. Is a leather fern. Tasty. (*chews on another*) Mmm-hmm. Mmm-hmm. That, folks, is alstroemeria. Not the best, but not the worst either. The worst? The worst are those flowers she brings home in the winter. Paper whites. Or, narcissus I think is what they're called. Awful. You can smell them from anywhere in the apartment! I know, I know, some people like them, you don't have to tell me. (*investigates another section of the flowers*) This over here, tastes like, a snapdragon. Common. But OK. It's a little too bitter for me. Oh, now this? This is a gerbera. These are very tasty. (*begins flicking his head harder*) Oh. I think I ate too much. Lots of fiber. Mmmmph! Roughage. Oh! That's gonna hurt.

*Shower turns off.*

## FLUFFY

Uh oh. She's coming. And something. Is stuck. In my teeth.

## DELILAH

(*from offstage*) Hey! Hey! Psssst! What are you doing? (*enters wearing only a towel, hair wet, holding a squirt gun*) What are you doing? Are you getting into my flowers?

## FLUFFY

Meow. I'm sorry. I couldn't help myself. You weren't here and I was just so…curious!

DELILAH

You know what they say about curiosity and cats.


FLUFFY

I do.


DELILAH

Don't (*squirts* FLUFFY) do that (*squirts again*) anymore (*squirt*)!


FLUFFY

Hey! What the - ! Are you kidding me?!


DELILAH

Fluffy, you're going to make yourself sick! Eating flowers! I like that location for the flowers so please just leave them alone. (*squirts him again*)


FLUFFY

Hey! I just wanted a taste. Honestly. I get no nature in this apartment so when you have fresh flowers, it's like being outside! In nature!


DELILAH

You don't like being cooped up in here, do you?


FLUFFY

("*no*") Meow.


DELILAH

What am I going to do? Let you go outside?


FLUFFY

Oh, I'd like that!

DELILAH

Fluffy, it's ghastly out there. You wouldn't like it, now would you?

FLUFFY

Yes, I would!

DELILAH

No, you wouldn't.

FLUFFY

Yes, I would!

DELILAH

You'd get lost. Or squashed flat by a car.

FLUFFY

I'd be fine!

DELILAH

I'm going to get dressed. Stay out of the flowers. I mean it (*squirts* FLUFFY *then goes into bedroom*).

FLUFFY

Hey! Meow! That was unnecessary! (*runs into bathroom, but after a moment, is apparently tossed bodily out of the bathroom; he lets out a long 'Meoooow!' This should be as spectacular as the actor can make it. Then, after a moment*) I don't appreciate that! (*hairdryer sounds from offstage*) And now I'm wet, got a full stomach. And I just got tossed! That's my bathroom, too! In case you forgot! I'm not a guest here! I'm just going to take a rest. Over here. (*He goes to couch and sits down.*) That lacked any sort of dignity, you know. I'm wet right here (*licks the spot*). And here (*licks another spot*). And I can feel I'm wet in other spots that I can't even get to. (*spins in a circle trying to reach the wet spot. Then, to* DELILAH) Not fair!

DELILAH

(*enters, dressing, sits on couch beside* FLUFFY, *still crabby with him*) What were you doing? Huh? What were you doing? You can't eat those flowers. You know that.

FLUFFY

I know that. Just trying to get some fiber in my diet.

DELILAH

Not good for your little tummy.

FLUFFY

Well, have you seen the food you give me? Do you look at it? Read the labels?

DELILAH

What's the matter? You don't like your food?

FLUFFY

Do you realize what would happen to you if that was all you ever ate? You'd be in the bathroom all day!

DELILAH

Your treats are good, aren't they?

FLUFFY

Yes, they're good. But I need some variety, OK?

DELILAH

(*cell phone rings*) Oh. Pepe.

FLUFFY

Oh, Pepe! I like him!

DELILAH

(*picks up, speakerphone or projection*) Hello Pepe!

PEPE

(*pronounces her name 'deh-lee-lah'*) Delilah! Mi amor!
What are you doing, baby?

DELILAH

Nothing. I'm just here. Home. What's up?

PEPE

Just wanted to know if you had breakfast yet?

DELILAH

I did. Fruit.

PEPE

(*offended*) What?

DELILAH

Not you, I had fruit. I ate fruit.

PEPE

Oh. Cos I was gonna bring you a croissant and a coffee.

DELILAH

Well, you could still do that.

PEPE

Oh, sí?

DELILAH

Yes, the fruit wasn't enough.

PEPE

Bueno, croissant and coffee. I'm right around the corner so
I'll be there in just a minute or two. Wait, you like cream and
sugar, right?

DELILAH

If they have oat creamer that would be supreme. No sugar.


PEPE

That's right. And not soy, yo recuerdo!


DELILAH

No soy.


PEPE

OK, ciao!


DELILAH

Bye.


FLUFFY

Should have asked for a bagel with smoked salmon.


DELILAH

I know. Didn't get you anything.


FLUFFY

Exactly! I'm always the first one you turn to but the last one
you think of.


DELILAH

Oh, come on. I still love you.


FLUFFY

Aw, I still love you, too. (*rubs his body on her*)


DELILAH

Hey, you're getting hair all over me.


FLUFFY

But listen, your mom is right. It's time to think about dating
again.

DELILAH

I like living here with you. Me, alone. My writing. My books. My life.

FLUFFY

But it would be nice to have someone to share it with, don't you think?

DELILAH

No one to pester me with questions.

FLUFFY

Think about the memories you could make!

DELILAH

No one to bother me.

FLUFFY

Might be nice to have someone else to make dinners for.

DELILAH

No one to make demands of my time.

FLUFFY

And what about…you know?

DELILAH

And do I really miss … *that*?

FLUFFY

Exactly! That's what I want to talk about! There are literally no other cats that come here! Ever!

DELILAH

And remember Dave?

FLUFFY

Didn't like him.


DELILAH

What a waste of food. (*imitating Dave*) 'Maybe we could, you know, keep it casual?' Men. Oh, and what's that song? By what's-her-name? Morissette? (*trying to remember Alanis Morissette tune*) 'All I need now is intellectual intercourse…' (*then sings while FLUFFY watches, terrified and in awe*) "And all I really want, is some justice! Oh, ay-ee-yi-ee-yi-yi-yeah!" (FLUFFY *doesn't know the song.*) You know, the 'jagged little pill' woman? That album was a blockbuster! I think they made a musical out if it, too. (*knock at the door*) Was that someone at the door? (FLUFFY *nods 'yes'; she waits a beat, then another knock, then she goes to the door.*) Oh, hi, Pepe.


PEPE

(*holds a bag containing two croissants and a drink holder with two coffees. He is slightly alarmed from the singing he heard in the hallway which was not unpleasant, just loud and intense.*) Hi?


DELILAH

Come on in.


PEPE

Are you ok?


DELILAH

Fine.


PEPE

Were you eh-singing?


DELILAH

I was.


28

PEPE

Oh, that was – good.

DELILAH

Thank you. You know, I do sing and I do get paid for it.

PEPE

I know. I heard you in the hallway. Alanis Morissette, right?

DELILAH

(*to* FLUFFY) See?

PEPE

Oh, sí! (*sings*) You've already won me over, in spite of me,

DELILAH and PEPE

don't be alarmed if I fall, head over feet!

DELILAH

Come in before the cat gets out. (FLUFFY *darts around*
DELILAH *and* PEPE, *dodges them both, and gets beyond
the door.*) Oh, no!

PEPE

Ay, Dios mío. Hold this (*gives* DELILAH *the bag and
coffees, brings cat back in any fashion they can manage:
over the shoulder, cradled in his arms, piggy-back, etc.*).
Come on, baby. You don't want to go out there!

FLUFFY

Yes, I do!

PEPE

(*playfully*) No, you don't. No, you don't.

FLUFFY

OK, but don't put me down. I like it up here.

DELILAH
Aw, look. Fluffy always liked you.

PEPE
Your creamer is in that bag.

DELILAH
Thank you so much.

PEPE
Don't mention it. (to FLUFFY) OK, you gotta get down now, baby. Ay, Dios! You got your claws in me! (*gets* FLUFFY *down*)

DELILAH
I'm going to just put it in the refrigerator.

PEPE
Oh, and I almost forgot, happy birthday!

DELILAH
Aw, thank you, Pepe.

PEPE
Belatedly, I mean. What did you do?

DELILAH
Fluffy and I got take-out.

PEPE
Aw, that's not enough to celebrate.

FLUFFY
Excuse me?

DELILAH
Eh, I couldn't think of anything to do. It's just a birthday.

PEPE

You should have called me!

DELILAH

I was happy to spend it with Fluffy.

PEPE

(*to* FLUFFY) Such a good boy. But you are getting big!
What is she feeding you?

DELILAH

Only what he'll eat.

PEPE

Really?

DELILAH

He's very picky. Oh, I almost forgot to ask. How was your
first date last night?

PEPE

Ay, qué cabrón!

DELILAH

What?

PEPE

Mira, it was nice. Up to a point.

DELILAH

Well, don't skip straight to the bad stuff, tell me all about all
of it! You brought coffee and croissants. Dish! (*They sit on
couch and spread out their breakfast on the coffee table, and
begin eating/drinking.*)

FLUFFY

Don't mind me. I'm just going to take a quick nap over here. (*stretches, finds a comfortable position*)


PEPE

So, we were to meet at 8 o'clock for appetizers and dinner at Joanina's. I get there right at 8 o'clock and wait. And wait. And I'm checking my phone and looking at the time and I tried to not order a drink because once I start, I don't want to just stop, entiendes?


DELILAH

Uh huh.


PEPE

So, I'm looking at my phone when a message pops up, and it says, 'Sorry it took me so long. Turn around.' So, I put down my phone slowly and I turn around and I was expecting to see someone right in front of me. But there was no one. Nadie. And then I see someone waving from, like, all the way across the restaurante. And I raise my hand a little like, 'eh?' Then I feel my phone vibrate and I look and it's another text and it says, 'Come over.' So, I started walking and I get closer and I realize that he has been sitting there the whole time. So I say, 'What happened? Why are you just sitting all the way over here by yourself? You change your mind?' And he says, 'I was nervous.' I thought about smacking him around piñata style, but I didn't. You would be proud of me: I took a deep breath and let it go.


DELILAH

Very good, Pepe.

PEPE

Mi amor. So, then I say, 'look, let's get a drink and then see how things go,' and he says, 'I don't drink.' So right there, that was a deal breaker for me but since I was trying to be nice, I said, 'Well, you could get a soda or something,' then he says, 'I'm not sure if this is right.' So I said, 'Derek, your name is Derek, isn't it? Well, let me say something to you, Derek: you are wasting my time!'

DELILAH

Oh, no!

PEPE

Oh, sí!

DELILAH

Poor guy.

PEPE

What do you mean, 'poor guy'? That was ridículo.

DELILAH

Oh, but come on, Pepe. Look – what did you say his name was? Derek?

PEPE

Sí. Derek.

DELILAH

So, Derek is just unclear on his preferences, and he got a little nervous.

PEPE

OK, being unclear about your preferences is OK when you're like, 16, but when you're my age? Please. You should have it figured out by now.

DELILAH

So many lost souls. Well, you said it was nice up to a point.
What was the nice part?

PEPE

Well, I was there! I got a drink – and the bartender's phone
number!

DELILAH

The bartender's phone number! But that means another date.

PEPE

Jah, another date. I'm OK with that. What else am I gonna
do?

DELILAH

You can't just be alone?

PEPE

I could. I suppose. But I need a partner in my crimes.

DELILAH

Well, bonne chance.

PEPE

Bonne chance? What is that? French?

DELILAH

Oui. Bonne chance. How do you say 'good luck' in Spanish?

PEPE

Buena suerte.

DELILAH

Ah, buena suerte - with your date.

PEPE

Gracias, mi amor! I think I'm gonna need it.

DELILAH

So, what brings you here?

PEPE

Oh, that's right. Delilah, I have a favor to ask.

FLUFFY

(*rousing himself to go over and hear the favor*) I heard that.
What's the favor?

DELILAH

Yes?

PEPE

Well, I had to take Carmelita to the vet today.

DELILAH

The vet? Oh, your poor kitty cat. How old is she now?

PEPE

I don't know. She's a shelter kitty. At least a year. Maybe a
little more?

DELILAH

And you had to take her to the vet?

PEPE

I think she ate something and then, well, it's kinda gross, but
she got worms or something. I really can't talk about it,
because just thinking about it makes me feel like I'm
gonna...

DELILAH

I get it, I get it.

FLUFFY

Hold on! You got some trashy shelter cat and now she's got worms? That is nasty.

DELILAH

That's not uncommon.

FLUFFY

Not uncommon for shelter cats maybe.

DELILAH

A lot of shelter cats will have residual issues like that. Fluffy was a shelter kitty.

FLUFFY

What?

PEPE

Your Fluffy was a shelter kitty?

DELILAH

Sure was.

FLUFFY

I was a shelter kitty?

DELILAH

And had worms when you were little, right?

FLUFFY

I had worms, too? Oh, sunny, sweet Je – !

PEPE

Anyway, she had also given herself an irritation on her back leg because she was biting it, so they put one of those cones on her neck.

DELILAH

A cone? Around her neck?

PEPE

Exactamente.

DELILAH

Oh, the poor thing.

PEPE

Sí, pobrecita.

FLUFFY

(*guffaws, then goes silent but still laughing*) Bwah-ha-ha!

PEPE

You probably could take the cone off, but you gotta watch
her and make sure she doesn't, you know, start chewing on
her leg or anything.

FLUFFY

(*audibly laughing, then fade as before*) Ahh-ha-ha-ha!

PEPE

Anyway, I have some things I gotta do and I wanted to know
if you could watch her for a few hours.

DELILAH

Today?

PEPE

Sí, hoy día.

FLUFFY

(*greatly alarmed*) What?

DELILAH

Oh, Pepe.

PEPE

What's wrong?

FLUFFY

What's wrong? I'll tell you what's wrong (*takes a deep breath as if he's going to explain*) –

DELILAH

Nothing, I just have to go out today for a little while, too.

FLUFFY

Yeah, Pepe, she has to go out.

DELILAH

You sure you can't just leave her in your apartment? And also, I mean, is whatever she has contagious?

FLUFFY

Wait, where you goin'?

PEPE

No, Carmelita is not contagious. I already give her the last of her medicine. And, mira, I'm gonna be gone hours chica; not just, 'a little while.'

DELILAH

Well, I do have to go out for a bit, but I won't be long. I'd have to leave them here alone but honestly, I don't mind if you don't mind.

FLUFFY

Why are you asking him if he minds? I'm the one that's gonna be here with Carmelita and her wormy bu –

PEPE

(*overlap first word*) But don't say you don't mind if you really do mind.

DELILAH

Truly, no big deal.

FLUFFY

Maybe for you.

DELILAH

And I'm sure Fluffy would like to have some company, wouldn't you, Fluffy?

FLUFFY

(*starts running around*) No! Please! No! I got to get out! Out!

DELILAH

Hey! Crazy cat! Cut it out! Come here (*she settles FLUFFY on couch*). Settle down.

PEPE

Aw, he's so cute. OK, sabes que te amo! Lemme go. I'll be right back with Carmelita. Ciao. (*sees himself out*)

DELILAH

Come here, baby. Let's talk. Come on.

FLUFFY

(*going to DELILAH*) Yeah, I want to talk with you, too.

DELILAH

(*scratches his head and under his chin*) You feel like some company today?

FLUFFY

("*no*") Meow.

DELILAH

You do?

FLUFFY

("*no*") Meow.

DELILAH

You have to be a good boy, OK?

FLUFFY

("*No, I don't*") Meow-yow.

DELILAH

Be nice, because Carmelita has a cone.

FLUFFY

("*Yes, I heard*") Meow. She also has worms, and I don't know if I want to be anywhere near her. Or her as –

DELILAH

As you heard Pepe, she's not contagious.

FLUFFY

That's what they always say. 'They're not contagious.' But guess what?

DELILAH

What is it, Fluffy?

FLUFFY

They are!

## DELILAH

Oh, stop it. Don't be such a drama queen. Hey, how about I brush you? Or a treat. You want a treat?

## FLUFFY

That would help.

## DELILAH

I'll get you a treat. (*gets treats, shakes the bag*)

## FLUFFY

(*bolts toward her*) Meow! (*gets treat, then goes up to his 'spot' by window*)

## PEPE

(*knock at door, then he enters holding* CARMELITA *who is wearing a cone*) Mira, Carmelita!

## DELILAH

Hi, Carmelita!

## PEPE

(*to* CARMELITA) You're going to stay with tía Delilah!

## CARMELITA

Meow?

## PEPE

Yes you are, yes you are! (*to* DELILAH) OK, gracias for taking Carmelita.

## DELILAH

Eh, cats are like potato chips. You can't have just one.

## CARMELITA

Meow?

DELILAH

Hello, Carmelita. Hey, baby!

CARMELITA

Meow?

PEPE

(*putting* CARMELITA *down*) OK, Carmelita. Hey, take your claws out of me! OK, Delilah, gracias so mucho (*air kisses* DELILAH)!

DELILAH

OK, Pepe. And thanks for the coffee and croissant – oh, and the 'tea' (*meaning 'gossip'*)! Most enjoyable.

PEPE

Claro! Ciao, baby! Ciao, to you, too my little Carmelita! (*kisses her, exits*)

DELILAH

(*with a sigh*) Maybe my errands can wait till tomorrow. Oh, tomorrow and tomorrow and tomorrow.

CARMELITA

(*beat*) Meow?

DELILAH

Hi, Carmelita. New surroundings, huh? You'll get used to it.

CARMELITA

Meow?

DELILAH

Where's Fluffy? Fluffy?

FLUFFY

(*whispers*) I'm up here.

DELILAH

Oh, Fluffy, there you are. Get down.

FLUFFY

(*continues whispering*) Shhh! I don't think she sees me!

DELILAH

Don't be ridiculous. (*goes to him*) Come on. (*he won't get down*) Oh, suit yourself. You two make yourselves comfortable. I'll be right back. (*exits to bathroom*)

CARMELITA

Meow? (*Unaware she's being watched, CARMELITA begins shaking her head from side to side, slowly at first, then more vigorously. When she realizes her efforts are not going to loosen the cone, she takes a break and thinks. She has an idea. She begins scurrying backwards on all fours doing a few circles around the coffee table, all in an effort to remove the cone.*) Meow?! Meeee-oooowwwwww!! Aye, madre mía! Socorro! Ay, ayúdame Dios mío! Get this stupid thing off me! Pepe? Pepe!? Dónde estás? Where are you? Pehhhh-paaaaaaayyyy!!! (*She tries to get the cone off using the sides of her hands, then her feet, but it's no use. She collapses on her back, exhausted.*) I hate my life.

FLUFFY

Aw, don't say that.

CARMELITA

(*with a hiss and a shriek, she jumps up*) Hssssstt! Mrrreeeooww! (*like cats growling at each other*) Wherrrrrrreee did yooooouuu commmme froooommmmmmm?

FLUFFY

Easy, now. Easy.

CARMELITA

(*still growling*) Wherrrrrrreee did yooooouuu commmme frooooommmmmmm?


FLUFFY

Oh, lord-a-mercy! I was just by the window. Please don't hurt me!


CARMELITA

How loooong were youuuuu (*speak these last words in a rapid, staccato fashion*) looking at me!?


FLUFFY

Not long, really. Really! I promise!


CARMELITA

Voy a matarte! I will kiiiiilllll youuuuuuu! How looooong were youuuuu (*again, very rapidly*) looking at me!?


FLUFFY

Uh, since you came in?


CARMELITA

You son of a biiiiiiiiiiiiii


FLUFFY

No, no! Look, you're in my house and I am trying to be hospitable. But you've got to calm down. You gotta calm down!


CARMELITA

Hssssstt! Mrrreeeooww!


FLUFFY

Easy, now, easy! What's your name? Carmelita, right? Carmelita?

#### CARMELITA
(*becoming less aggressive*) Hssssstt! Posible. Y, cómo te llamas?

#### FLUFFY
Uh, Fluffy.

#### CARMELITA
(*gives a sharp 'hssssstt' then cocks her head to the side; she pronounces his name with a vowel sound in front, as in, 'eh-fluffy'*) eh-Fluffy?

#### FLUFFY
Yeah. Fluffy. What's wrong with that?

#### CARMELITA
You don't look muy eh-Fluffy to me.

#### FLUFFY
Yeah, we're all aware of that. I'm not very fluffy, but my name is Fluffy. So, Carmelita, huh?

#### CARMELITA
Sí. Carmelita.

#### FLUFFY
Well. That's a lovely name.

#### CARMELITA
(*begins to ease*) Oh. Gracias.

#### FLUFFY
And it suits you.

#### CARMELITA
You think so?

FLUFFY

Yes. And, uh, your fur is beautiful and shiny. You must really take care of yourself.


CARMELITA

Well, yes. I do.


FLUFFY

And, and, the way you wear your, uh, cone is very –


CARMELITA

My cone? My cone!?


FLUFFY

Wait a minute, now. Wait a minute!


CARMELITA

My cone!?! Hijo de un cerdo! [Son of a pig!] MrrrreeeeeeooooOOOOOWWW!!! (*she launches at* FLUFFY; *they tear around the room*)


DELILAH

(*entering*) What in the world is going on in here? Hey, hey, hey! Stop it! Right now!


FLUFFY

She started it.


CARMELITA

(*to* DELILAH) No te metas dónde no te llaman! [Don't interfere where you are not called/wanted.]


DELILAH

What's the problem?


CARMELITA

Mrrrreeeeeeooooo OOOOOWWW!!!

FLUFFY
Yeeeoowww! She's doing it again!

DELILAH
Hey, hey! Pssst! Stop it! I mean it!

CARMELITA
Wrrrroooowwwww.

DELILAH
Come on.

CARMELITA
Wrrrroooowwwww.

DELILAH
Easy there, girl. Come on, what happened?

CARMELITA
Ese gato. Meeeooowww! He was not being nice!

DELILAH
(*concerned*) Carmelita, I can't understand you when you're
so upset. What are you saying?

CARMELITA
He was not being nice!

FLUFFY
What are you talking about?

CARMELITA
He was teasing me about my cone!

DELILAH
Were you teasing her about her cone?

FLUFFY

What? No! I said it looked nice on her!

CARMELITA

Meeerrroww!!

DELILAH

Easy, there.

FLUFFY

I did! I said, the way you wear your cone is –

CARMELITA

Yes! 'The way you wear your cone!' Cone, chico! As if I have a choice! And that is not nice, Mister eh-Fluffy!

FLUFFY

Hey, hey! There's no 'mister.' It's just 'Fluffy', OK?

CARMELITA

O, sí, 'just eh-Fluffy, OK'!

DELILAH

Is this true? Were you teasing her about her cone?

FLUFFY

Well. I really didn't mean for it to be teasing. I was just trying to be complimentary about her in general. And in doing so, I happened to mention her cone.

CARMELITA

Meeerrroww!

DELILAH

Hey, hey!

FLUFFY
Because it's around her neck, right there in front of me!

CARMELITA
Me estoy calentanda, chico. [You're making me angry, boy.]

DELILAH
What was that?

FLUFFY
I think she's mad.

DELILAH
Now, Fluffy. Remember when you had to wear a cone?

FLUFFY
Oh, please don't bring that up.

CARMELITA
You had a cone?

DELILAH
You hated it, didn't you?

CARMELITA
You had a cone?

FLUFFY
OK, fine. Yes. I had a cone and I hated it!

DELILAH
So, why don't we all just start over, OK? OK?

FLUFFY
(*"OK"*) Meow.

CARMELITA

(*"OK"*) Meow.


DELILAH

Good. Now. You two just sit right here and I'll get you both some treats, OK?


FLUFFY

(*"OK"*) Meow.


DELILAH

You?


CARMELITA

(*"OK"*) Meow.


DELILAH

Good (*goes to get treats*).


FLUFFY

Listen, I'm sorry about what I said. I didn't mean to give offense.


CARMELITA

OK. No preocupes. Está bien. [Don't worry. It's OK.]


FLUFFY

Does that mean we're cool?


CARMELITA

Sí. Cool. (*beat*) And that is a nice collar.


FLUFFY

Oh, this? Thank you. (*going to scratching post*) And look, why don't you come over here and try this first class scratching post out. This will make you feel better in no time!

CARMELITA
(*scratches on the post a few times*) Ay, que bueno! Oh, yes!
Yes! Sí, sí, sí!

FLUFFY
(*intrigued by how much* CARMELITA *is enjoying the post,
goes over to her, bends down and begins aiming his nose at
her butt*) Meow?

CARMELITA
Hey! What are you doing?

FLUFFY
Meow.

CARMELITA
(*pushes his face away*) Get away from my butt!

FLUFFY
Just trying to get to know you a little better.

CARMELITA
You are so rude!

FLUFFY
(*offers his butt*) OK. You go first.

CARMELITA
Ay! Move it! I'm not interested!

FLUFFY
Hey, I was just trying to demonstrate friendship and trust.

CARMELITA
Mira, we just met. You can't come on so strong like that.

FLUFFY

Oh, sorry.


CARMELITA

I just want a few more minutes with this post. Alone.
(*resumes scratching*) Ay, Sí, sí…sí!


FLUFFY

(*watches as* CARMELITA *finishes scratching on the post,
and is mesmerized as she slinks to a new spot and begins
grooming herself. Then, to the audience*) My life has
changed. My life. Has changed. (*to* CARMELITA) Oh, and I
just wanted to say, these treats she's about to give us? They
are top notch!


DELILAH

(*returning*) Here you go. One for you and – hey!


FLUFFY

(*overexcited, he jumps for the treat but pulls back and lets*
CARMELITA *have first one*) My bad. You go first.


CARMELITA

(*finishing up*) Mmmmm. Qué delicioso!


FLUFFY

Right? (*eats his*)


DELILAH

Oh, Carmelita. You look so uncomfortable.


CARMELITA

Meow.


DELILAH

Is that cone bothering you?

CARMELITA

Meow.

DELILAH

Pepe did say I could take it off. (*begins removing*
CARMELITA'S *cone*) You behave. No biting yourself, OK?

CARMELITA

O, so much better! Muchas gracias señorita! (*licks her arm
then begins biting it*)

DELILAH

Ah! Ah! I said no biting! No biting! (CARMELITA *opens
her mouth intent on biting her own arm, they all freeze for a
moment*) I'll put the cone back on you!

CARMELITA

(*defeated*) Ay, caramba.

DELILAH

Now, look. I need you two to get along. I have bills to
organize and pay, my mother is coming over – my mother is
coming over! (*realizing the horror, the judgment of her
mother*) I've got to vacuum.

FLUFFY

We got to hide! We got to hide!

> CARMELITA *hunkers down, sensing that
> something bad is about to happen.*

FLUFFY

(*from a 'safe' spot*) Over here! Come over here!
(CARMELITA *runs to* FLUFFY.)

> DELILAH *goes to bedroom and reappears with*

*vacuum going full blast. The sound and action of the vacuum is terrifying to both* FLUFFY *and* CARMELITA. *When* DELILAH *finishes vacuuming,* FLUFFY *and* CARMELITA *have worked themselves into a panting, open-mouthed state of shock.*

DELILAH

OK. That'll do. (*puts the vacuum away*)

CARMELITA

What was that?

FLUFFY

A vacuum. She uses it to clean the carpets. What? You don't have a vacuum in your house?

CARMELITA

(*taking deep breaths*) No carpets. Hardwood floors only. He sweeps. You got a valium or Xanax or something? Just tell me where it is and I'll get it.

FLUFFY

Maybe I do. But I'm not gonna tell you.

CARMELITA

What? Why not?

FLUFFY

I'm a cat, not a dog.

CARMELITA

(*thinking*) Cat, not a dog? What does that have to do with anything?

FLUFFY

If I was a dog, I would tell you. Since I'm a cat (*shrugs*).
See, dogs give all their human's secrets away. In fact, they
got dogs that are designed specifically for pointing out the
drugs. You see them at airports, in line-ups. But, cats? Cats
don't tell anyone where anything is, ever. Especially the
drugs.

CARMELITA

Something is loco with you.

DELILAH

(*returning*) Now, I don't need you two fighting, understand?

FLUFFY

No fighting. We're way past that. You should see her at the
scratching post.

CARMELITA

(*to* FLUFFY *"stop it!"*) Meerooww! (*to* DELILAH) And no
more vacuuming, por favor!

DELILAH

Did you enjoy your treats?

FLUFFY and CARMELITA

(*"More treats?"*) Meow?

DELILAH

What? More treats?

FLUFFY and CARMELITA

(*"More treats?"*) Meow?

DELILAH

Ah! You two are killing me. No more treats, you greedy little
—

**FLUFFY and CARMELITA**
(*"More treats?"*) Meow?


**DELILAH**
No treats. You both are gonna get too big to leave the house.


**CARMELITA**
(*starts to 'meow' but stops short*) Mee –. Did she just call us 'fat'?


**FLUFFY**
No, no. She was talking about how, uh, big and strong we are from all this, uh, exercise.


**DELILAH**
I know, Fluffy. How about I get your box of toys?


**FLUFFY**
Toys?!


**DELILAH**
You could share your toys with Carmelita, right?


**CARMELITA**
Did she say 'toys'? As in, juguetes?


**FLUFFY**
Oh, yeh-heh-heeeessss!


**DELILAH**
(*Returning with a box of toys including a mouse, ball with a bell inside, an inflated balloon, and a large yarn ball that unravels*) OK, here you are! Mom should be here soon, I suppose. You two play and I'll pick up a bit.


*Upbeat, fun music here.*


56

FLUFFY *and* CARMELITA *begin to play.*
*NOTE: Avoid putting toys in mouth. This section*
*should be choreographed to suit the abilities of*
*the actors. Take only one item out of the box at a*
*time. The mouse is first.* FLUFFY *passes the*
*mouse to* CARMELITA; *she plays for a bit, then*
*passes mouse to* FLUFFY *so that he can have a*
*turn. They bat the toy back and forth for a while*
*then decide to select another toy.* CARMELITA
*reaches in and pulls out a ball with a bell inside.*
*Again, they have their turns playing with the toy.*
*Next,* FLUFFY *takes out the balloon. Perhaps*
*let this action move into the audience so that*
*they can play, too. After a short period of time,*
FLUFFY *or* CARMELITA *should bring the*
*balloon back on stage. Last is the ball of yarn*
*that unravels. Initially,* CARMELITA *and*
FLUFFY *might look disappointed with such an*
*'old-school' toy; but when it begins to unravel as*
*they play, they are excited. Make a mess. Have*
*fun.*

DELILAH
(*entering, stunned,* FLUFFY *and* CARMELITA *freeze when*
*they see her*) What. Is going on here? Fluffy! Carmelita!
What did you do? (FLUFFY *and* CARMELITA *slowly back*
*away toward the upstage area and into a makeshift hiding*
*place near or behind the couch*) How was this possible?
Mother is going to be here any minute and look at the place!
You two are both in big trouble. (*she begins cleaning the*
*mess*)

FLUFFY and CARMELITA
Meow?

DELILAH

Not a word!

FLUFFY and CARMELITA

Meow?

DELILAH

From either of you!

FLUFFY and CARMELITA

Mee –

DELILAH

Tssshht! (*still cleaning*) Unbelievable. I was out of the room, what? Five minutes? Not even! (*knock at the door*) I'll be right there!

NANCY

(*from outside*) It's me. Delilah?

DELILAH

Just a sec, ma!

NANCY

Are you OK?

DELILAH

(*opens door*) Am I OK?

NANCY

(*enters holding a bag with clothes, some knick-knack figurines, leftover snacks and dark chocolate, a notebook of music, and a second bag which holds a bowl-shaped aquarium filled with water and a beta fish*) You didn't answer the door, I was worried.

DELILAH

Ma, I'm OK. I just needed a sec.

NANCY

What happened in here?

DELILAH

Nothing, I – the cats got into a box of toys.

NANCY

Cats? Did you say cats?

DELILAH

Yes, cats. There are two cats here.

NANCY

Not just Fluffy?

DELILAH

Yes, plural, 'cats' as in, not-just-Fluffy.

NANCY

I didn't know you had another cat.

DELILAH

I don't. I'm just watching Pepe's cat, Carmelita, for a spell.

NANCY

I don't see them.

DELILAH

That's because they are hiding. (*dramatic*) They are loathe that I should find them.

NANCY

They are what?

**DELILAH**

They're in big trouble, ma, they're in big trouble.

**NANCY**

They did all this?

**DELILAH**

No. I'm redecorating. (*as in, "do you like it?"*) What do you think; tell me you like it?

**NANCY**

It's different.

**DELILAH**

Never mind.

**NANCY**

Lilah, you should get out more. Maybe meet a man.

**DELILAH**

The only thing a woman should hope for, right ma?

**NANCY**

(*not listening*) And I brought you some clothes to try on and if you don't like'em, I can return'em because I kept the receipts!

**DELILAH**

I'll look at them in a minute, let me put these things away.

**NANCY**

There are a few tops in there that are mine but I don't wear them anymore, so you can have'em.

**DELILAH**

Ah. One woman's refuse is another's treasure.

NANCY

You might like'em.

DELILAH

That's true. I might like'em.

NANCY

Also wanted to give you the music that Ariana and Anthony want for their wedding.

DELILAH

What is it?

NANCY

The usual. Oh, and I brought you these sea salt dark chocolates because I can't have them in the house.

DELILAH

(*incredulous; she understood what* NANCY *said*) Brought what?

NANCY

You like dark chocolate, right?

DELILAH

Yes, but I don't want it in my apartment either.

NANCY

But I thought you liked dark chocolate.

DELILAH

I do. And I like pepperoni pizza, cheesecake, and parfait, but I don't keep those stashed in the fridge! (*looks at some of the clothes* NANCY *brought, holds one up, maybe goes into bathroom to look at it*)

NANCY

All right, so you can give them to Father Ryan when you see
him at the wedding today. I just don't –

DELILAH

Today? The wedding is today?

NANCY

Yes, I told you that on the phone.

DELILAH

No, mother, you didn't!

NANCY

I did, when I asked you!

DELILAH

You said – I don't recall exactly what you said, but you most
certainly did not say 'today'!

NANCY

All right. Well. Can you sing at a wedding today?

DELILAH

I have so much to do!

NANCY

What are you doing?

DELILAH

I have bills, I have cleaning, writing; I'm watching Pepe's
cat.

NANCY

Which I still don't see. Fluffy either.

DELILAH

Give them time. Like me, they have to muster courage when you visit.

NANCY

Oh! Here he is! (*goes to pet him*) Hello, Fluffy! Hello! (FLUFFY *sees an insect and begins chasing it*) Delilah? Delilah? What is he doing? Looks like he's chewing on something.

DELILAH

(*occupied with looking through clothes*) Oh, no! Does he have a bug?

NANCY

I don't know.

DELILAH

Ma, don't let him have it! It'll make him vomit!

NANCY

I'm not letting him have it, he's having it himself!

DELILAH

(*rushing over*) What is it? What do you have? Argghhh. It is a bug. Great. Did you eat it?

FLUFFY

(*becoming nauseous*) Meow.

DELILAH

Now you're going to wretch somewhere, aren't you? Aren't you? Little turkey.

FLUFFY

Meow!

NANCY

Is that what makes them throw up?


DELILAH

I don't know, mom. Any number of things makes a cat
'throw up.'


FLUFFY

Meow!


NANCY

I don't know how you stand it. One instance of puke and that
cat would be out the door!


DELILAH

It's a wonder I made it through babyhood in your house.


NANCY

What do you mean?


DELILAH

Well, I feel certain that at some point when I was a baby, I
must have gotten ill and – what was it you said? 'Puked.'


NANCY

Oh. Well, when babies throw up, it's different.


DELILAH

Yeah, when babies do so, it's all over your shirt, all over
your clothes; when cats heave, it's on the floor.


NANCY

No, what I'm saying is that when a baby throws up, you
don't mind because it's your baby.

DELILAH

Well, when a cat vomits, I can't imagine that it's that much different than if it were a baby doing the same.

NANCY

That's something about having pets I will never understand. It's a cat. It's a dog. It's not a baby.

CARMELITA

(*coming from behind couch*) Meow!

NANCY

Oh! Here she is!

DELILAH

Carmelita.

CARMELITA

Meow!

NANCY

Oh, hi, Carmelita! Do you speak Spanish, like Pepe?

CARMELITA

Meow!

NANCY

I don't know, that sounded like English, to me.

CARMELITA

Merrrrooowwww!

NANCY

Uh oh! Sounds mad!

DELILAH

Oh, she's fine. Calm down, Carmelita.

NANCY

(CARMELITA *begins putting her paws on* NANCY) No,
no! You're not getting on me! I don't want cat hair all over
me.

CARMELITA

Oye, chico. Quién es? [Hey, boy. Who is that?]

FLUFFY

Oh, her? That's Delilah's mom, Nancy.

DELILAH

What time is the wedding?

NANCY

Four o'clock.

DELILAH

And why is it that you can't sing at this wedding?

NANCY

I have an appointment.

DELILAH

Chiropractor?

NANCY

How did you know?

DELILAH

That much you told me on the phone.

FLUFFY

I was a witness!

NANCY

But that's not till later.

FLUFFY

I was a witness to that, too!

NANCY

This afternoon, I wanted to see Louise and Maryellen for lunch. Remember, Louise…

NANCY and DELILAH

is moving at the end of the month,

NANCY

– right, and this is the only time she can get together.

DELILAH

Fine.

FLUFFY

Hold on, you're singing at that wedding today?

DELILAH

Today.

FLUFFY

So, you're gonna be gone?

DELILAH

Looks like I'm definitely going to be out.

CARMELITA

Estaremos solos? [We're going to be alone?]

NANCY

What do you mean?

DELILAH

Just thinking out loud.


NANCY

Don't do that. I can hardly understand when you're just
speaking regular. What are you saying?


DELILAH

Well, I had thought I would run some errands but then Pepe
brought Carmelita over, then I thought I would just stay here
and be with the cats, do some writing, but now it looks like
I'm singing at a wedding so I'm definitely going to be out
whether it be doing something for myself or a favor for you.


NANCY

Well, thank you.


DELILAH

You're welcome.


NANCY

You <u>are</u> getting paid.


DELILAH

And the music?


NANCY

The usual; they're doing "here comes the bride, there goes
the bride," and the Ave.


DELILAH

The Ave? Seriously?


NANCY

I know.

DELILAH

Who's playing?

NANCY

Barbara.

DELILAH

Oh, mom.

NANCY

What?

DELILAH

Barbara cannot transpose. She can hardly play.

NANCY

She's a volunteer.

DELILAH

Who cannot transpose.

NANCY

Why would she need to transpose?

DELILAH

Because "Ave Maria" is in B flat and it sits better in my voice in A flat.

NANCY

Look, if my lunch with Louise and Maryellen is short, then I could probably sing the Ave with you.

DELILAH

Fine.

FLUFFY

(*the vomit is coming, begins heaving*) Weeehh – hehhh.

NANCY

What's he doing?

FLUFFY

Weh -hehhh. Eehhh-hehh.

NANCY

Delilah?

FLUFFY

Weh -hehhh.

DELILAH

Great, he's going to vomit. (*moving* FLUFFY *to uncarpeted area*) Get off the carpet, you!

FLUFFY

Weh -hehhh. Eehhh-hehh. Heehhh! Heeehhhh!! (*then, finally*) Woollllrephhh!

NANCY

Oh my god.

DELILAH

Oh, Fluffy!

NANCY

Oh, god.

DELILAH

Well, at least you did it on the floor and not on the rug (*quickly cleans mess with paper towels and spritz*).

NANCY

I think I'm going to be sick.

CARMELITA
No, I think I'm going to be sick!

NANCY
I need to go to your bathroom.

DELILAH
Be my guest.

CARMELITA
Oh, let me go first! (*but* NANCY *gets to the bathroom first and closes the door on* CARMELITA'S *face*). Ay, bruja! Miércoles de la semana! [Witch! Wednesday of the week! *NOTE: considered a mild curse phrase because the first syllable in 'Miércoles' is the first syllable of a stronger Spanish curse word.*]

DELILAH
(*to* FLUFFY) Naughty little beast.

FLUFFY
Leave me alone. I couldn't help myself. Had to get that up. Oh, I still don't feel so good.

CARMELITA
Mira, hombre. Es culpa suya. [Look, dude. It's your own fault.]

DELILAH
(*goes to* CARMELITA) Oh, poor Fluffy. What do you think, Carmelita?

CARMELITA
Meee – yow.

DELILAH
Hmm? What do you think, Carmelita?

CARMELITA
(*not irritated with* DELILAH; *rather, reinforcing*) I said,
meow. It's his own fault.

DELILAH
It's his own fault, right?

CARMELITA
Sí. Dije que no debe comer ese insecto. Estúpido. [Yes. I said
that he shouldn't eat that insect. Stupid.]

DELILAH
Shouldn't have eaten that bug, right?

CARMELITA
Claro! That is what I say!

DELILAH
Every time he eats bugs he gets sick.

CARMELITA
Sí. Ya lo sé. [Yes. I already know.]

DELILAH
Why don't you listen to Carmelita, Fluffy?

CARMELITA
Exactamente! Por qué no me escuchas? [Exactly. Why don't
you listen to me?]

DELILAH
(*sits beside* FLUFFY, *trying to comfort him*) It's really too
bad, Fluffy.

CARMELITA
Es una lástima, chico. [It's a shame, boy.]

## DELILAH

And you do this all the time. Do you know the definition of insanity? Hmmm? It's doing the same thing over and over again and expecting a different result.

## CARMELITA

Ha! See? You are insane! Loco!

## DELILAH

You'd think he'd learn and not do such foolish things, right Carmelita?

## CARMELITA

Ah, sí! Estoy de acuerdo con esta mujer. [Ah, yes! I am in agreement with this woman.]

## FLUFFY

Leave me alone.

## CARMELITA

Tú eres tonto o...barres playas? [Are you stupid or... do you sweep beaches?]

## DELILAH

Maybe it's some sort of punishment for cats. Did you wrong the god of the cats somehow? Hmm? That you keep doing the same thing over and over and expect a different result? Does this make you happy to vomit like this?

## CARMELITA

(*continues poking fun at him*) Jah! You do the same thing over and over and expect a different result! Are you happy?

## FLUFFY

Why are you two against me right now? Didn't you see what just happened?

CARMELITA
We saw it. I wish I could un-see it; but we saw it.

DELILAH
Aw, Fluffy. Are we teasing you too much?

FLUFFY
All I know is, I just got sick in front of everybody. (*beat*) I'm
so embarrassed.

CARMELITA
Dijo que tiene vergüenza. [He said that he is embarrassed.]

DELILAH
What did he say?

CARMELITA
Vergüenza. Dijo que tiene vergüenza. He is embarrassed.

DELILAH
But I bet you won't do that again!

NANCY
(*returning*) Oh. I still feel faint.

DELILAH
Ma? Are you OK?

NANCY
I'm fine. I hope you're happy, Mr. Fluffy.

CARMELITA
Jah! I hope you're happy, señor eh-Fluffy!

FLUFFY
Oh, somebody save me! I'm being yelled at by three women!

NANCY

I just about lost my breakfast in there.

FLUFFY

Well, I lost my breakfast – and all those treats! I'm gonna be so hungry now.

DELILAH

I'm sure you're going to be hungry now that you lost all your breakfast.

FLUFFY

Meow.

DELILAH

I suppose I could give you a little food.

CARMELITA

No, gringa, don't give him any food!

NANCY

You're going to give him food?

CARMELITA

Let him learn a lesson! Digo que le dejes sufrir! [I say let him suffer!]

FLUFFY

Whose side are you on?

DELILAH

Well, what am I going to do? Never feed him again?

FLUFFY

Oh, please don't even say that!

NANCY

He's your cat.

DELILAH

But no treats!

FLUFFY

No treats?!

DELILAH

No treats.

FLUFFY

There is no justice.

CARMELITA

But I can have treats, sí?

DELILAH

The only one that's being a good kitty is Carmelita.

CARMELITA

Ah, bueno!

DELILAH

She can have treats.

CARMELITA

(*very excited, dances and sings a la "Macarena", freezes after each of her lines so the others can speak*) 'Dale a tu cuerpo –' [Give happiness to your body – ]

DELILAH

You want a treat, Carmelita?

CARMELITA

'– alegría, las botanas!' [ - happiness, treats!]

                    DELILAH
Stay right there, I'll get you a treat.

                    CARMELITA
'Dale a tu cuerpo alegría, las botanas!'

                    DELILAH
(*returning*) Here you go!

                    CARMELITA
'Eh, las botanas, ay!'

                    NANCY
Your cats…(*others slowly turn and look* at NANCY) are
psychotic.

                    DELILAH
Oh, come on. They're fun! You know, in ancient times, cats
were revered among the gods.

                    CARMELITA
Especially the female cats.

                    NANCY
Yes, and today, they scratch up the furniture and puke all
over the house. I have to go. Thank you for doing the
wedding. I'm sorry I interrupted your plans for the day.

                    DELILAH
I could use the money, right?

                    NANCY
Who couldn't?

                    DELILAH
Exactly.

NANCY

I'll try to make it to the wedding in time for the Ave Maria.

DELILAH

I'd appreciate it.

NANCY

And if you decide you don't like any of those tops, I will take them back so you don't have to.

DELILAH

OK. Thanks, mom.

NANCY

I've gotta go. Goodbye, Fluffy.

FLUFFY

Meow.

NANCY

Goodbye, Carmelita.

CARMELITA

Adios.

FLUFFY

They don't understand Spanish.

CARMELITA

What are you talking about? Everybody understands 'adios,' chico.

FLUFFY

I mean, 'meow' is more comprehensible to them.

CARMELITA

O, por favor. Mira. Adios, Señora Nancy!

NANCY

Did she just say 'goodbye, Nancy?'

FLUFFY

See? Didn't understand.

CARMELITA

Yes, she did!

DELILAH

I believe so.

NANCY

Pepe's cat, right?

DELILAH
Pepe's cat.

NANCY

(*clears throat and then, a little too loudly*) Adios, Carmelita!

CARMELITA

Ah – ha! (*to* FLUFFY) No sabes ni papa de algo, chico!
[You don't know anything about potatoes, boy!] She's
learning! Adios, señora! Que tenga un buen viaje!

NANCY

She said something, I'm sure; but I don't know what.

CARMELITA

I said, have a nice trip!

NANCY

Eh, no idea. When foreigners come into the country, they
should be required to learn English.


CARMELITA

(*to* FLUFFY *and* DELILAH) I don't think I like her too
much anymore.


DELILAH

But when you travel to other countries, you shouldn't have
to learn any foreign languages, right ma?


NANCY

When I travel? I'm not traveling.


DELILAH

Of course you're not. You embody the provincial.


NANCY

I'm not sure what you're talking about.


DELILAH

The predictability of our dialogue.


NANCY

Oh, and I almost forgot. Look! I got you some more of those
figurines you like.


DELILAH

Figurines?


NANCY

Yeah, the glass figurines you used to collect?


DELILAH

When I was eight, mother.

NANCY

Here, look (*pulls out four or five small glass figurines and places them on the coffee table*). They're all ocean animals.

DELILAH

So they'll match. (*veiled sarcasm*) Mother, you think of everything.

NANCY

Oh, and there's a toy for Fluffy in that bag.

FLUFFY

A toy? Just for me?

NANCY

You'll have to share with Carmelita.

FLUFFY

What?

DELILAH

Oh, thanks, mom.

NANCY

Are you being sarcastic?

DELILAH

Not at all. You're very thoughtful.

NANCY

I wish I could stay to see you open it, but I gotta go. Oh, and there's one other gift in that big bag for Fluffy for when you're gone.

DELILAH

What is it?

NANCY

A beta fish.

DELILAH

A beta fish?

NANCY

So he'll have something to look at when you're away!

DELILAH

A beta fish for while I'm away.

NANCY

Yeah, what's the problem?

DELILAH

You don't see how that's going to be a problem?

NANCY

No problem.

DELILAH

Even a minor problem?

NANCY

What? Fish are hypnotizing and soothing! That's what that doctor on the radio says.

DELILAH

Well, if that doctor on the radio says so then it must be so.

NANCY

OK, goodbye! And, adios, Carmelita!

CARMELITA

(*takes* NANCY *by the arm and walks her to the door, speaks the following with false sincerity.* FLUFFY *is the only one who can understand* CARMELITA *here*; NANCY *should just smile and nod, completely baffled*) O, adios vieja! Pienso que estás mas loca que una cabra! O, sabes que yo no tengo pelos en la lengua y hablaré sin rodeos! Ya, adios! Adios, vieja loca! [Goodbye old lady! I think you are crazier than a goat! Understand that I don't mince words and I will speak frankly! Yes, goodbye! Goodbye, old crazy lady!] (*closes the door, turns to* FLUFFY) OK, you were right. She doesn't speak Spanish.

DELILAH

A beta fish. Honestly? (*puts the beta fish on the dining table, then, as a warning*) Just because it's on the dining table does not mean that it's for dinner. All right, you two. I'll get you some more food and then I need to get ready to sing at this wedding (*gets more food for* FLUFFY). Behave. (*begins to exit toward bedroom*)

FLUFFY

Meow? Meow?

DELILAH

What? Your food is right there.

FLUFFY

Meow?

DELILAH

I don't want to go through this charade again. You don't like your food? Don't eat it.

FLUFFY

Meeeoooowww!

CARMELITA
You are loco! Just ask her, chico!

FLUFFY
All right. Could I have the toy?

CARMELITA
Manners, chico!

FLUFFY
Could I please have the toy?

DELILAH
Oh! You want your toy?

CARMELITA
See?

FLUFFY
Meow! I mean, yes!

DELILAH
OK, let's see what she brought (*opens package - it's an automated, interactive cat toy that has a feathery 'lure' attached*). Ooo! This looks fun! (*begins opening toy*)

CARMELITA
Que…es…este?

FLUFFY
I don't know, but I am very, very, very curious…

DELILAH
I'll turn this on, but then I have to go. Do not destroy the place!

*Fun, upbeat music here.*

DELILAH *turns on the toy and exits.*
CARMELITA *plays with it first while* FLUFFY
*watches, trying to not be interested. After a few
moments,* CARMELITA *pulls* FLUFFY *over so
they can both play. After they have exhausted the
toy, they begin to just play with each other. They
play together in various ways: joyfully,
competitively, flirtatiously, etc. Find a place in
the music for them to – in a compromising
position – come to a sharp stop; panting, out of
breath.*

FLUFFY

Oh, uh. Pardon me.

CARMELITA

(*composing herself, with dignity*) It is ok. It is ok. No
preocupes. [Don't worry.]

FLUFFY

Maybe we should take a break. Before things get too…

CARMELITA

Sí. A break. I am a little…hot.

FLUFFY

Yes, you are. I mean, I am, too. Hot. It's hot. Up here.

CARMELITA *fixes her clothes. Adjusts her top. Flicks her
hair. Gives a long, sensual stretch, sashays to couch and lies
down in her most smoldering manner.*

FLUFFY

(*to audience*) Oh, hi. I think now's a good time to, uh. You
know. Take a break. I mean, she's hot. We've been playing
and, uh, we need to cool off.

## CARMELITA

Mister eh-Fluffy…?

## FLUFFY

(*turns to face* CARMELITA) Yes, Carmelita?

## CARMELITA

(*beat, then sensually*) Meow.

## FLUFFY

(*mouth wide open, turns slowly back to audience, mouths 'Oh, my gosh!'*) Ladies and gentlemen, we're gonna take a short break right now. Y'all do the same. We'll all come back in a little bit, refreshed and, uh, relieved!

<u>End of Act I</u>

ACT II

## Scene 1

SETTING: *Same as ACT I. A few hours after the events of ACT I. At rise,* FLUFFY *and* CARMELITA *are sitting in the windowsill.* DELILAH'S *cell phone is on the coffee table.*

FLUFFY
What I'm saying is, if you have hope, then you have defeated the punishment of the gods.

CARMELITA
I still don't understand. What is this 'punishment of the gods'?

FLUFFY
I'm talking the ancient gods, like Zeus or Jupiter.

CARMELITA
Understood. OK, continue.

FLUFFY
Oh, you know. That life is suffering and all that.

CARMELITA
But is life really suffering? I mean, we got it pretty good, no?

FLUFFY
For now. But you're gonna die one day.

CARMELITA
Hey, nine lives, señor eh-Fluffy. Nueve. Vidas.

FLUFFY
Oh, you don't believe *that* do you?

CARMELITA

Why not?

FLUFFY

That's just an old wives' tale. Superstition.

CARMELITA

Es una posibilidad. [It's a possibility.] But I'm counting on nine lives during my one lifetime.

FLUFFY

But even then, you'll die after your so-called nine lives.

CARMELITA

I will be satisfied then.

FLUFFY

Oh, you will, will you?

CARMELITA

Claro que sí. [Clearly, yes.]

FLUFFY

That's what everybody says. But then when a person has what they've been wishing for, guess what?

CARMELITA

What?

FLUFFY

They're not happy. They want more. And that's what I see all the time. People spending so much time trying to figure out how to live a second lifetime when they don't even know what to do with the one life they've been given.

CARMELITA

Uh-huh. Wait. Let me fix your collar (*does so*). Better. It's really nice.

FLUFFY

Thank you. Again.

CARMELITA

OK, muchacho, let's get back to defeating the gods. How do we do that?

FLUFFY

Hope. It's like I said.

CARMELITA

How do you come to that?

FLUFFY

Well, to tell you about that, I have to tell two stories. One at a time. The first story is about a Greek man, the second is about a French man.

CARMELITA

Greek man. French man. OK. Venga. [Come.]

FLUFFY

All right. You know about Sisyphus?

CARMELITA

Sissy who?

FLUFFY

Sisyphus. He was a very wise man.

CARMELITA

I don't know many wise men.

FLUFFY

Well, he was a wise man.

CARMELITA

Ha! On whose authority?

FLUFFY

On the authority of a lot of people! Now, you can't interrupt me or I'll never get through this.

CARMELITA

Ay, jai – jai! Tranquilate, chico. [Calm down, boy.]
Solamente estoy asking a question. Dime. [Tell me.]

FLUFFY

All right. So, Sisyphus was a very wise man. A crafty man. Clever, and cunning.

CARMELITA

Bueno. Continue.

FLUFFY

And he wanted to defeat death.

CARMELITA

Defeat…death.

FLUFFY

Well, more precisely, he didn't want to die; and in order to not die, he thought he would have to defeat death. Or at least, defeat the personification of death. You follow?

CARMELITA

OK, so, if death is defeated, then there's…what? Only life?

FLUFFY

Exactly. And not only would Sisyphus not die, but everyone else would not die. There would be only life.

CARMELITA

Ah, bueno! I'm liking this Greek Sisyphus hombre.

FLUFFY

So, to do this, Sisyphus manages to trick certain gods. Now, there are a few different versions of this part of the story. One goes that Sisyphus chained up a guy named Thanatos so that he couldn't take Sisyphus or anyone else to the Underworld. During this time, no one died.

CARMELITA

Exactly who is Thanatos?

FLUFFY

Thanatos is basically the personification of Death. So, when Death cannot do his duty, well, everybody lives.

CARMELITA

Lucky for them, no?

FLUFFY

The other version is that Sisyphus chained up Hades himself so that he couldn't take anyone to the Underworld; and again during this time, no one died. Hades is the –

FLUFFY and CARMELITA

– god of the Underworld.

CARMELITA

Again, this is suerte [luck] for them!

FLUFFY

But in either case, whether it be Thanatos or Hades, he is
freed and eventually people begin dying again.

CARMELITA

And when either one was freed, he must have been pretty
angry con Sisyphus.

FLUFFY

Yes. Very angry.

CARMELITA

So, que pasó? [So, what happened?]

FLUFFY

Sisyphus was punished for his trickery by Zeus and Hades.

CARMELITA

How?

FLUFFY

He was forced to roll a boulder up a hill for all eternity by
Zeus and then Hades made it so the boulder would always
slip at some point and roll back down the hill.

CARMELITA

So, he would never get the boulder to the top of the hill?

FLUFFY

You understood before I said it. Yes, he would never get the
boulder to the top of the hill. And so –

CARMELITA

And so, he had to go back and get it over and over again and
roll it up the hill over and over again.

FLUFFY

Precisely.

CARMELITA

That is ridículo. A meaningless task. Why doesn't he just stop?

FLUFFY

It's a myth. A legend. It's his punishment. He can't just stop. The gods are making him do it. And the meaninglessness of his task is meant to be an example of the daily routines we go through. The meaninglessness that life can at times present.

CARMELITA

Jah, yo comprendo. The meaninglessness of life. (*looks out window*) Like, look at those people out there. What are they doing? Where are they going? To their jobs? The grocery store? Doing the same thing over and over again? And that traffic? Dios mío. And what is the point?

FLUFFY

Exactly. It can all begin to feel absurd.

CARMELITA

This is quite a myth.

FLUFFY

It's meant to teach a lesson.

CARMELITA

Like what? Don't try to cheat death?

FLUFFY

That. And a lesson that pertains to my second story.

CARMELITA

That's right. The second story. The French man?

FLUFFY

The French man.

CARMELITA

You're quite the little philosopher, Mister eh-Fluffy.

FLUFFY

Oh, yeah. We cats are natural philosophers.

CARMELITA

(*beat*) You ever get a craving for grass?

FLUFFY

A craving for what?

CARMELITA

Grass, man, grass. You know. Some really good grass.

FLUFFY

Oh, yeah. I tried those flowers over there earlier.

CARMELITA

Not the same, right?

FLUFFY

Not the same.

CARMELITA

Yeah. Some grass would be really good right now. I don't
mean some weed either. That stuff is nasty.

FLUFFY

Bitter, right?

CARMELITA

Exactamente. Bitter.

FLUFFY

Now you're making me crave grass!

CARMELITA

That would be so good. We could roll it. Chew it. So good. OK, OK. Let's get back to your story.

FLUFFY

Where were we?

CARMELITA

Let's see, Sisyphus, rolling a boulder up a hill over and over again, absurdity, don't try to cheat death…

FLUFFY

Ah, yes! And how that leads to the second story and the French philosopher.

CARMELITA

Sí, the French philosopher. But you gotta excuse me for a momentito, cos I need to clean a spot on my arm (*begins cleaning her arm, this should be mildly distracting for* FLUFFY).

FLUFFY

OK, so the French philosopher's name is Camus.

CARMELITA

Camus?

FLUFFY

Yes, Albert Camus.

CARMELITA

All these funny names.

FLUFFY

Just different.

CARMELITA

Sí, de acuerdo! [Yes, I agree!] I'm just saying they are a little funny, I'm not giving offense!

FLUFFY

Anyway, Camus came up with a story about Sisyphus to explain how to be at peace – even happy – with our lives.

CARMELITA

Ah, you see! You said 'lives'! That is plural!

FLUFFY

No, no. What I mean is –

CARMELITA

Nueve. Vidas. Chico. Plural.

FLUFFY

What I mean is Camus came up with an approach to being – to existence – that helps to accept our life as it is. Our singular life, as it is.

CARMELITA

Bueno. Ándale.

FLUFFY

Essentially, Camus suggests that if Sisyphus could perform his task of rolling the boulder up the hill incessantly – I mean, over and over again –

CARMELITA

I know what 'incessantly' means, chico.

FLUFFY

OK, OK. So, Camus suggests that if Sisyphus could perform
his task of rolling the boulder up the hill over and –
incessantly – he must do so with a certain mind set. A
condition.

CARMELITA

Yes, the condition. I'm listening.

FLUFFY

You just seem like you're not listening.

CARMELITA

Chico, I am cleaning. You think looking like this doesn't
require a little effort?

FLUFFY

(*beat*) I could help.

CARMELITA

You could help?

FLUFFY

With your cleaning.

CARMELITA

You want to help me with my cleaning?

FLUFFY

I'm really good! (*moves close to her, tongue out*)

CARMELITA

You. Wish.

FLUFFY

No, really, I could. Especially those hard to reach places?

CARMELITA

Te la estás buscando, chico. [You are looking for it, boy.]
Meee—rrrrowww!!!

FLUFFY

Hey, hey! OK. I got it. Yo comprendo. (*tries again*) But right
there…

CARMELITA

Ay, no te soporto, chico (*gets down from windowsill*). [I can't
put up with you.]

FLUFFY

Wait, wait! Don't go. Come on. Hey. Let me finish my story.

CARMELITA

OK. But only because I want to defeat death. Finish your
story down here. And mind your own business. (*by this time,
they are both by the coffee table, curious about the glass
figurines*)

FLUFFY

OK. Now, I forgot where I was. (*during this section,
FLUFFY and CARMELITA begin pushing the figurines
back and forth and off the coffee table*)

CARMELITA

You were saying that Camus says that Sisyphus must roll the
boulder up the hill, but with a condition.

FLUFFY

Ah, yes! The condition. The condition was that Sisyphus
must roll the boulder up the hill, but he must do so with joy.

CARMELITA

Roll the boulder up the hill…with joy?

FLUFFY

Joy!

CARMELITA

(*flatly*) Joy?

FLUFFY

Or at least, be happy. That's it! We must think of Sisyphus as a happy man.

CARMELITA

I don't know about a boulder, but I'm happy pushing these glass thingys.

FLUFFY

And that's the way Sisyphus must be!

CARMELITA

Wait a minute, wait a minute. So, you're gonna tell me that this French guy, Camus, wants Sisyphus to be happy while rolling the boulder up the hill over and over again?

FLUFFY

Yes. Because if he is happy while performing a punishment set forth by the gods, then he shows hope, even defiance… and –

CARMELITA

– he will have defeated the gods.

FLUFFY

Yes!

CARMELITA

Yes.


FLUFFY

And his life will not be meaningless. Because he is living his
life – no matter how tedious, repetitive and difficult as it
might be – but with hope and as a happy man! For us, it
would be as a happy cat.


CARMELITA

But this is what it means to be a cat, amigo! Everything we
do is with joy! Watch this (*pushes a figurine off the table,
they laugh*).


FLUFFLY

Oh, let me try! Let me try! (*pushes a figurine off table,
laughter again*)


CARMELITA

See? Joy!


FLUFFY

Yeah, I know! That is why you don't need nine lives to be
happy! Just the one.


CARMELITA

Just the one. (*beat*) Still, it must be hard for Sisyphus.


FLUFFY

Well, Sisyphus was a very strong man so he could manage
that boulder with no problem.


CARMELITA

O, dame paciencia. [Oh, give me patience.] I'm not talking
about his strength and pushing the boulder, chico. I'm
talking about him being alone.

DELILAH

(*bursting into the room partially dressed to sing at the wedding – bra and skirt? Whatever is appropriate for your venue*) Where's that notebook of music?

CARMELITA

(*arching her back and hissing*) Hssssttt! Ay cielos! (*another hiss*) Me asustaste! No sabía que estabas aquí todavía! [Oh hey! You scared me! I did not know you were still here!]

DELILAH

Oh, sorry, Carmelita! I didn't mean to scare you. Here, let me get you a treat.

CARMELITA

Ah, bueno! A treat! This is all you had to say!

FLUFFY

Hey, what about me!

DELILAH

Oh, you can have one, too. Try to keep it down, Mister Fluffy!

CARMELITA

Ha! See? You are 'Mister eh-Fluffy'!

DELILAH

(*sees figurines on the floor before she gives treats*) Hey! What happened here?

FLUFFY

It was her idea.

CARMELITA

Hey!

DELILAH

These are glass! They'll break!

CARMELITA

I thought you didn't like them.

DELILAH

They could break and then there's glass on the floor and you could get glass in your paws – not to mention my feet. You two aren't going to like this, but I'm going to have to run the vacuum again.

CARMELITA

Wait – did she say 'vacuum'?

FLUFFY and CARMELITA

Meee – Nooooo! (*they scatter, DELILAH picks up the figurines and runs vacuum over the area, then returns it to the bedroom area*)

DELILAH

I suppose you still want treats?

FLUFFY and CARMELITA

Meow! Meow!

DELILAH

Oh, fine (*gives treats, sits with them, but only FLUFFY eats his treat. CARMELITA noticeably hides hers behind her back*). You two are quite a pair. And is that a gray hair on you, Fluffy?

FLUFFY

(*"No"*) Meow.

### DELILAH

Oh, Mister Fluffy. I guess we're all getting older. Here, let's put these out of harm's way; like … in the garbage! (*gives them both a kiss on the head, tosses figurines in kitchen garbage, and then returns to her bedroom with the sheet music*).

### FLUFFY

(*following DELILAH as she goes to garbage*) But your mother gave you those!

### DELILAH

They're junk!

### FLUFFY

They're fun to push off the table!

### DELILAH

I don't care!

### FLUFFY

(*dejected*) Meow.

### CARMELITA

Excuse me. Mister eh-Fluffy? Mister eh-Fluuuuuuuffy?

### FLUFFY

What is it?

### CARMELITA

(*sensual, teasing*) You haven't had your treat yet. (FLUFFY *goes directly to* CARMELITA, *sits, and gazes at her*.) No, no. Not me. Look down. (*treat is on the floor; she is offering her treat to* FLUFFY)

### FLUFFY

Oh! Gracias.

CARMELITA
(*begins to mildly flirt with him*) So, 'Mister eh-Fluffy'?

FLUFFY
Don't bring that name up again.

CARMELITA
What? That you are really, 'Mister eh-Fluffy'?

FLUFFY
I'm too busy with this treat to be bothered arguing with you.

CARMELITA
Why argue, Mister eh-Fluffy?

FLUFFY
Look, 'Mister Fluffy' sounds too old. Like my dad.

CARMELITA
What's wrong with being old? Isn't that the goal in life? To
eventually be old?

FLUFFY
I suppose.

CARMELITA
And besides, 'Mister eh-Fluffy' sounds distinguished; not
old.

FLUFFY
Listen, I've been doing the whole 'Fluffy' thing for so long,
I'm not sure if I can add the 'Mister' to the front of it.

CARMELITA
It's not so hard, Mister eh-Fluffy.

FLUFFY

Look, if I'm going to add a prefix to my name, I think I've earned a Ph.D. by now. (*clears throat, tests it out*) 'Doctor' Fluffy.

CARMELITA

(*becoming sensual*) No, no. Not 'doctor'. Mister eh-Fluffy. Mister eh-Fluffy is better. (*beat*) There's a spot. Just on the back of my neck. Could you scratch that?

FLUFFY

Uh…OK (*does so to the delight of* CARMELITA, *she starts to purr*).

CARMELITA

Muchas gracias, Mister eh-Fluffy.

FLUFFY

Are you…purring?

CARMELITA

What? It feels nice.

FLUFFY

(*after a moment*) Why don't we, um, go back to the window and see what's going on? (*springs to windowsill*) Did you know I almost caught a bird today?

CARMELITA

(*slowly slinks over*) What do you mean you 'almost caught a bird today'?

FLUFFY

I did. That bird came so close.

CARMELITA

Mister eh-Fluffy. There's a window. You can't get a bird
through the window.


FLUFFY

I said, 'almost.' 'Almost'! Oh, oh! Look! There's birds out
there now!


CARMELITA

Dónde?


FLUFFY

There!


CARMELITA

O, mira! Palomas.


FLUFFY

What?


CARMELITA

Pigeons! I hate those things. Nasty.


FLUFFY

Rats with wings, right?


CARMELITA

I hate rats, too. Son sucios. [They are dirty.]


FLUFFY

What?


CARMELITA

Dirty. Sucios. They are dirty. (*beat*) What is it about scales
and feathers?

FLUFFY

I don't know. But just the thought of scales and feathers on other creatures makes me want to kill, kill, KILL!

CARMELITA

Ay, cálmate, chico! You're going to scare them away. Oh, here they come. Oh, if only – (*sees that* FLUFFY *is getting ready to pounce*) what are you doing? There is a window there? You not gonna get it!

FLUFFY

I can try. Here it comes (*jumps at bird*)!

CARMELITA

Más tonto y no naces. [Any stupider and you wouldn't have been born/made it out of the womb.]

FLUFFY

What?

CARMELITA

This is why you don't have a Ph.D.

FLUFFY

A what?

CARMELITA

There's a window there, genius.

FLUFFY

So?

CARMELITA

Forget it.

FLUFFY

Come on. Tell me you weren't tempted to jump.

CARMELITA

Jah, OK, chico. But otra vez [again]: there is a window right there.

FLUFFY

I might have gotten lucky.

CARMELITA

You would like to get lucky, wouldn't you? (*beat*) Don't look at me like that.

FLUFFY

Like what?

CARMELITA

(*moving toward beta fish on table*) You know how you're looking at me.

FLUFFY

And I know how you're looking at that fish.

CARMELITA

Right?

FLUFFY

Don't do it.

CARMELITA

Don't do what?

FLUFFY

What you're about to do.

CARMELITA

Come here and help me get this thing.

FLUFFY

It's in water. I hate the water.

CARMELITA

That's why I want you to help me.

FLUFFY

Help you? More like, get it for you.

CARMELITA

That would be nice. Come on. Ayúdame. (*They begin dipping their paws into the water, their backs turned to the audience as* DELILAH'S *cell phone begins ringing startling both* FLUFFY *and* CARMELITA. *They quickly turn around, looking very guilty.*)

DELILAH

(*mostly dressed for the wedding, she enters the main area as her cell phone continues ringing*) Ah! Pepe! (*on speakerphone or projection*) Pepe? Hi!

PEPE

Delilah! Mi amor! Cómo estás?

DELILAH

I'm fine, Pepe. I thought you'd be back by now. Where are you?

PEPE

Food shopping. I went home and realized I had nothing to eat!

DELILAH

You're at the grocery store now?

PEPE

Sí.

DELILAH

I could use a grocery shop. There's not a thing in the house that will satisfy me.


PEPE

What do you need, baby? I'm here.


FLUFFY

What are they talking about?


CARMELITA

(*garbled, since she has a mouth full of beta fish*) Not sure.


DELILAH

(*notices* CARMELITA *has an odd sound to her voice*) Eh, it's too much for me to ask. I'll just do a grocery shop later. But you know what you could do?


PEPE

Dime. [tell me]


DELILAH

Hold on a second. Carmelita? What's in your mouth?


CARMELITA

(*garbled*) Meow.


PEPE

What's going on?


DELILAH

Carmelita has something in her mouth.


PEPE

Oh, no!

#### DELILAH

Carmelita? What's in your mouth?

#### CARMELITA

(*garbled*) Meow.

#### DELILAH

Where's the fish?

#### FLUFFY

I didn't do it.

#### DELILAH

Carmelita, did you eat the fish?

#### CARMELITA

(*garbled*) Meow.

#### DELILAH

Oh, for the love of –

#### CARMELITA

(*swallows with a gulp, then clearly says*) Meow!

#### PEPE

What is happening?

#### DELILAH

How do you feel about Carmelita eating fish?

#### PEPE

Oh, that's OK. It's fish.

#### DELILAH

Good. Because she just did.

CARMELITA

Meow!

PEPE

Is that my baby?

DELILAH

Yes, it is. And she just solved a minor problem for me.

PEPE

A minor problem?

DELILAH

Never mind. Listen, about groceries. You could get me a
coffee creamer. One of those oat creamers?

PEPE

Oh, sí. But isn't there a lot of sugar in those things?

DELILAH

Pepe, I don't care. It's the way they are made. I don't think
it's possible for it not to come with added sugar.

PEPE

But the soy doesn't have added sugar.

DELILAH

Yes, I know. But my mother has gotten it into my head that
soy mimics estrogen and causes complications for women,
so...

PEPE

I don't think that it's soy that's causing complications for
women, mi amor.

DELILAH

Well said, Pepe.

PEPE

OK, I think there are only a couple of flavors for the oat creamer. Which one do you want?

DELILAH

The vanilla. Or hazelnut. Whatever they have that will transform my coffee into a liquid candy bar.

PEPE

Mira, if you want a liquid coffee candy bar, you should just go to Starbucks.

DELILAH

My own oat creamer will do, thank you.

PEPE

OK. But escucha, anything else? Do you have some food for dinner?

DELILAH

I don't know. To know would require a trip to the kitchen. No, I don't think so.

PEPE

Delilah. Did you look?

DELILAH

I always do.

PEPE

What is it? Are you short on money?

DELILAH

My bank account is an embarrassing testament to my choice of occupation.

PEPE

Oh, Delilah! Let me get you something!

DELILAH

Pepe. Love. I couldn't bear the thought of creating an inconvenience for you.

PEPE

It is no inconvenience, Delilah.

DELILAH

(*has an idea*) I've got it. Pepe.

PEPE

Sí?

DELILAH

A solution.

PEPE

Jah, I'm listening, dime! [tell me]

DELILAH

Let's dine out.

PEPE

You and me?

DELILAH

Yes! Tonight! Unless you think it's rash.

PEPE

Like, on a date?

DELILAH

Oh, Pepe. I didn't think I was your flavor.

PEPE

Listen, if you like liquid coffee candy bars, then you're my flavor!

DELILAH

This changes the evening entirely!

PEPE

Oh, this makes me so happy!

DELILAH

And let me treat you, yes?

PEPE

I thought you say you don't have no money.

DELILAH

I'm fine, I'm fine. I'm singing at a wedding. I'm sure they'll give a good tip.

PEPE

Oh, now I'm really happy! You gonna spoil me!

DELILAH

I simply must get out of this apartment. And not just to go out to sing at somebody else's wedding.

PEPE

Oh, Delilah, you sound a little down. But listen, we're gonna have fun tonight, OK?

DELILAH

I always do. With you.

PEPE

Aw. OK, so, how's my little Carmelita?

DELILAH

Except for eating my fish, she's an angel.


PEPE

Can she stay a little longer?


DELILAH

Of course. You can take her home after our entanglement
tonight.


PEPE

'Entanglement'?


DELILAH

Our date, Pepe. Our date.


PEPE

Perfecto. OK, I'm gonna finish food shopping, get your
creamer, then I gotta wash the city off me, and I will pick
you up at 7:30, OK?


DELILAH

Yes, please do wash the city off. If there's one thing I can't
stand it's a filthy gay man.


PEPE

I won't be filthy, Delilah.


DELILAH

Well, maybe just a little.


PEPE

Stop it.


DELILAH

See you then.

PEPE

OK, ciao! (*air kiss over phone*)


DELILAH

Ciao. (*ends call*) You two hear that? I'm going out after the wedding. (*finishes dressing by now, begins getting her other things together*)


FLUFFY and CARMELITA

Meow?


DELILAH

I'll be back. I'll feed you then. Relax.


FLUFFY and CARMELITA

Meow?


DELILAH

Where are my – ? Oh, forget it. I'll take a Lyft.


FLUFFY and CARMELITA

Meow?


DELILAH

Keys. Phone. Music. Excellent. Very well. Goodbye, my loves! Behave.


FLUFFY and CARMELITA

Meow?


DELILAH

Fluffy, you be good to Carmelita while I'm gone, yes?


FLUFFY and CARMELITA

Meow?

DELILAH

You two are high maintenance, you know that?

FLUFFY and CARMELITA

Meow?

DELILAH

Goodbye, goodbye, parting is such sweet sorrow. (*exits, locks door on other side*)

> FLUFFY *and* CARMELITA *sit side by side watching the door for an extended beat.*

FLUFFY

Meow?

CARMELITA

Shhh!

FLUFFY

(*beat*) Meow?

CARMELITA

Tssshhhttt!!

FLUFFY

(*longer beat*) Meooow?

CARMELITA

Ay, callate la boca! How are we gonna hear if she's coming back if you keep making all that noise?!

FLUFFY

(*distraught*) She ain't coming back. This part is so hard. She might not ever come back.

CARMELITA

Would you relax, chico? She's gonna be back.

FLUFFY

Just reminds me of when I was little.

CARMELITA

When you were little?

FLUFFY

Uh – huh. My mama left me. And never came back.

CARMELITA

Aw, Mister eh-Fluffy. Your mama didn't leave you. It's people. They take little kitties away and put them in different homes.

FLUFFY

They do?

CARMELITA

Sí.

FLUFFY

Wait. So, it wasn't her choice? My mama was taken from me?

CARMELITA

Well, I suppose you could say that. Or you could say that you were taken away from your mama. Either way, you two got separated but it's only because people wanted to put you in different homes.

FLUFFY

Yeah, but I was put in a shelter.

CARMELITA

Mira, I was put in a shelter, too. And it was hard. But look at
you now. You're in a nice home. That Delilah is a lovely
lady. She gives you treats, scratches your back. You gonna be
OK, Mister eh-Fluffy (*she starts pulling lint off the back of
his neck and shoulders*).


FLUFFY

What are you doing?


CARMELITA

You've got some fuzzies in your fur back here.


FLUFFY

Oh. Thank you. I mean, gracias.


CARMELITA

Come over here and sit down (*they go to couch, she
continues grooming him*). Put your head in my lap. Close
your eyes. (FLUFFY *protests*) Shhhhh. Cierra los ojos, close
your eyes. You have your own boulder, don't you? Hmmm?
Being alone is your boulder. My little Sisyphus. You've been
pushing that boulder of being alone up the hill for so long,
haven't you? Only to have it roll down every time. Every
time.

> *As the lights and mood shift,* PEPE *appears on a
> platform just outside the window in a dazzling
> singer's costume. He begins playing "Poesía"
> on his guitar (see appendix for music) or other
> Spanish style lullaby.* CARMELITA *continues
> grooming* FLUFFY *for a while, then they stand
> and dance.*

PEPE (*sings*)
QUÉ ES POESÍA, POESÍA QUÉ ES? UNA FRASE, UNA
IDEA, UN CURSO DE CORAZÓN?
ES LA LUZ EN TUS OJOS, LA LUZ EN TU CARA, LA
LUZ EN TU CUERPO, LA LUZ EN TU ALMA

LOS SUSPIROS SON DE AIRE Y VAN AL AIRE, LAS
LÁGRIMAS SON AGUA Y VAN AL MAR
DIME, MUJER, CUANDO EL AMOR SE OLVIDA

SABES TÚ A DÓNDE VA?
SABES TÚ A DÓNDE VA?

> *As the song ends, the scene transitions back to
> the way things were,* PEPE *disappears from the
> window.* FLUFFY *is asleep on* CARMELITA'S
> *lap. She strokes his head. It's a sweet, intimate
> picture. But then* FLUFFY *begins to snore. It's
> endearing at first, but* CARMELITA *becomes
> displeased as* FLUFFY'S *snoring becomes
> louder and more obnoxious.*

CARMELITA
Ay, dame paciencia, Dios. [God give me patience.] (*she
pushes* FLUFFY *onto the floor*)

FLUFFY
(*wakes abruptly*) Yo, motherf- I didn't do it! I didn't do it!
Police brutality! Police brutality! Don't taze me! I am not
resisting arrest! I am not –

CARMELITA
Cálmate, mi amor, cálmate.

FLUFFY
I didn't do it! I didn't...(*regains his bearings*) I didn't...do
it. (*beat*) Did I?

CARMELITA

No. You didn't do it. (*raises an eyebrow*) And neither did we.
(*They find new positions in the room*) What I don't
understand is this whole captivity thing. I mean, look.
There's a big world out there! I want to stretch my legs! Take
a look around! Listen to good music, eat good food, and
drink good bebidas!

FLUFFY

I used to feel like that.

CARMELITA

'Used to'?

FLUFFY

Yeah. I would run out of the apartment and almost make it
outside. But then I'd get nervous and by that time, Delilah
would snatch me up.

CARMELITA

Maybe you're just not fast enough.

FLUFFY

Oh, I'm fast. I just got…a little…uh…

CARMELITA

Scared?

FLUFFY

Yeah. OK? I got scared.

CARMELITA

Aw, my little scaredy cat.

FLUFFY

But I still try to overcome it every once in a while.

CARMELITA

Oh?

FLUFFY

That's right. Every once in a while, when Delilah opens the door, I try to run out and see how far I can get. I figure, the farther I go, the more I conquer my fear.

CARMELITA

I think I figured you out.

FLUFFY

How's that?

CARMELITA

You don't meditate enough.

FLUFFY

I don't meditate at all.

CARMELITA

See? That's the problem. All cats meditate. And you're acting like a dog.

FLUFFY

I don't act like a dog.

CARMELITA

Yes, you do. You keep looking for acceptance and trying to please people. You let them do whatever they want and pretend like that's OK. They have to earn your respect, you don't just give it to them for no reason. Makes them think they can do whatever they want and you'll still approve of them.

FLUFFY

That sounds conditional. Like conditional love.

CARMELITA

If you want to call it conditional then it's conditional. My point is, we all have to work on our relationships. You don't just tell someone you love them once and then never say it again. You don't just show someone you love them once and then never do it again. We all need reminders. Verbal and physical.

FLUFFY

Oh, I like those reminders. (*walks toward her, eagerly*)

CARMELITA

(*makes a fist*) Here's a reminder, chico.

FLUFFLY

(*backing down*) OK, ok. I always thought you were supposed to love unconditionally.

CARMELITA

Who said that?

FLUFFY

Some man at Delilah's church.

CARMELITA

Well, it might have been some man at Delilah's church, but let me tell you something.

FLUFFY

What?

CARMELITA

That man at Delilah's church was never married.

FLUFFY

How do you know?

CARMELITA

Because he clearly doesn't understand love, chico.

FLUFFY

So, marriage is 'conditional'?

CARMELITA

Jah, it is. It's all conditional. If someone tells you different,
they're lying or just fooling themself. You not gonna love
someone who doesn't treat you right. That's ridículo. We've
evolved. Treat others the way you want to be treated. And
that, my friend, is conditional. So don't be a dog. Be smart.
Be a cat, my little philosopher.

FLUFFY

Cats are smarter than dogs.

CARMELITA

You don't have to tell me.

FLUFFY

Right?

CARMELITA

I mean, you can't get eight cats to pull a sled through the
snow. (*beat*) You know? Eight cats? Pulling a sled through
the snow? What? I'm just saying. Look, just be yourself.
Just…be.

FLUFFY

Just be.

CARMELITA

Yes. Just be. And breathe. Here, let me help you relax. You got a spot on your back that needs cleaning. I'll get it. (*starts, stops*) But don't get the wrong idea, OK? (*no contact need actually be made, she begins cleaning his back with her tongue, as cats do*)

FLUFFY

Oh, yes. OK, yes. That's the spot.

CARMELITA

Easy, cowboy.

FLUFFY

Don't stop. (*she resumes*) Yeah. I couldn't reach that. (*beat*) You know, Delilah is very much into meditation and yoga and all that.

CARMELITA

(*actor or director can decide when* CARMELITA *should stop grooming* FLUFFY *during this sequence*) Oh, sí?

FLUFFY

She even became a vegetarian. Maybe vegan.

CARMELITA

What is that? Vegan?

FLUFFY

Well, it's like being a vegetarian except it's more strict.

CARMELITA

More strict? So, not just not eating meat and that sort of thing?

FLUFFY

Right. So, as a vegan, you wouldn't eat any product that came from animals.

CARMELITA

Like butter, cheese, milk?

FLUFFY

Nope. Wouldn't eat those things. Some vegans don't even eat honey.

CARMELITA

Yeah, but does honey really come from bees?

FLUFFY

Sure, it does.

CARMELITA

I mean, I know bees make honey, but it's not like it comes out of their bodies, does it?

FLUFFY

Their mouths. I think.

CARMELITA

Their mouths? OK, I don't want no bug spit, even if it is sweet.

FLUFFY

Anyway, it's a product of that creature's efforts.

CARMELITA

Huh. That's very…considerate. But I couldn't do that. I love fish. And cheese and chicken! So good. Especially when they are put together! I don't think I could be a vegan.

FLUFFY

I don't think I could either.


CARMELITA

We need those oils and proteins for our fur and muscles.


FLUFFY

People don't have fur and muscles. Maybe that's why they can be vegans.


CARMELITA

Oh, but people have muscles.


FLUFFY

They do?


CARMELITA

Claro. It's just that some of them don't use them. Like cats? We use our muscles all the time. People? Not so much.


FLUFFY

(*sees something by window, bolts*) Meeerrreeooowwww!!


CARMELITA

What is wrong with you? You gonna crash through that window and then you'll really know what it's like to be outside!


FLUFFY

There's a fly in here.


CARMELITA

Una mosca?


FLUFFY

A fly, a fly!

FLUFFY *tears around the room trying to catch the fly.* CARMELITA *watches the scene he is making. Finally, she reaches out calmly and snatches the fly in mid-air with her hands and slaps it onto the ground.*

FLUFFY

Hey! Let me have that.

CARMELITA

No.

FLUFFY

Come on, please! Let me have it!

CARMELITA

No! You gonna eat it and make yourself sick and I can't watch that again.

FLUFFY

Let me have it! I won't eat it, I promise!

CARMELITA

No. Now, listen to me. I'm gonna put it under the couch.

FLUFFY

What?

CARMELITA

And you better not try to get it. (*she bats it under the couch*)

FLUFFY

Aw, what'd you do that for?

CARMELITA

Is this what you do all day when Delilah is not home? You run around and eat bugs?

FLUFFY
Maybe.

CARMELITA
Ay, Dios mío. Men. You are so simple sometimes.

FLUFFY
What?

CARMELITA
Men are so simple.

FLUFFY
What do you mean, 'men are so simple'?

CARMELITA
Look at you. You're chasing a bug around the apartment.
You just about destroy the place trying to catch it. And when
you do catch a creature, you wanna kill it and eat it.

FLUFFY
It's the hunter instinct in me.

CARMELITA
It's the stupid instinct in you, is what it is.

FLUFFY
Hey, now. That's not being very nice.

CARMELITA
I'm not trying to be nice, I'm just trying to keep you from
throwing up all over the place. And now, there's no one here
to clean it up. (*beat*) And don't look at me. I'm not gonna
clean it up!

#### FLUFFY
I'm never going to live that down, am I?

#### CARMELITA
Not as long as you keep trying to eat bugs, no! (*as he sulks*)
Ay, jai, jai! Don't be such a boy.

#### FLUFFY
And what about girls?

#### CARMELITA
(*sassy*) I don't see any girls here. Do you?

#### FLUFFY
Oh, excusez-moi. Women.

#### CARMELITA
Ah, women.

#### FLUFFY
And this whole equality thing, I mean…(*thinks she might be offended*) you know…

#### CARMELITA
Women who seek to be equal to men lack ambition.

#### FLUFFY
No, no. What I mean is, women can't do the same things that men can.

#### CARMELITA
Women don't *want* to do the same things that men do.

#### FLUFFY
But what I mean is…

CARMELTIA

Eh, muchacho. To stop digging the hole, you gotta first put down the shovel.


FLUFFY

(*beat, figures out her meaning*) Oh. I see what you mean.


CARMELITA

Just be glad you are here. If, as you said, for only one lifetime. Especially since you are here with me.


FLUFFY

I am glad.


CARMELITA

And realize that you owe it to a woman.


FLUFFY

How's that?


CARMELITA

Chico. Everything born on this earth comes from a woman.


FLUFFY

Huh. I never thought of that.


CARMELITA

You should think of it.


FLUFFY

(*considering this new fundamental observation*) Everything born on this earth comes from a woman.


CARMELITA

Mmm-hmm.

FLUFFY

(*beat*) Except maybe seahorses.

CARMELITA

Seahorses?

FLUFFY

Yeah! Seahorses. The male seahorse has the pouch and gives birth to the little baby seahorses.

CARMELITA

Seahorses.

FLUFFY

Yeah, you know (*does an imitation of a seahorse*).

CARMELITA

Seahorses is the exception you cling to in order to dismiss the point of what I am saying?

FLUFFY

Just a tidbit of information that I thought might interest you.

CARMELITA

You thought that might interest me?

FLUFFY

Am I wrong?

CARMELITA

I'll let you figure that out on your own.

FLUFFY

Women can just be…confusing to me, sometimes.

CARMELITA

There's no confusion.

FLUFFY

No confusion?


CARMELITA

No confusion.


FLUFFY

I beg to differ.


CARMELITA

I'll make it simple for you: everything that is worth doing in this lifetime, whether it be having coffee in the morning, going on vacation, having a glass of wine, watching the sunset, going for a walk; anything you can think of, women make it better. They add beauty. Class. Elegance. And we inspire love.


FLUFFY

Oh, yeah?


CARMELITA

Sí, caballero. Go to any museum and do you know what form is the most painted? The female form. And, why? Because women add beauty. Class. Elegance. And inspire love.


FLUFFY

Beauty. Class. Elegance. And –


FLUFFY and CARMELITA

Inspire love.


FLUFFY

(*taking her hand, crossing downstage*) I feel all romantical… and inspired. (*strikes a classical acting pose*) If I profane with my unworthiest hand –

CARMELITA

Oh, no, no, no.

FLUFFY

If I profane with my unworthiest hand this holy shrine,

CARMELITA

Holy shrine. Ay.

FLUFFY

– the gentle sin is this, my lips, two blushing pilgrims, ready stand to smooth that rough touch with a tender kiss. Come on. Do your part.

CARMELITA

Chico, I –

FLUFFY

(*gently, picking up where he left off*) With a tender kiss…

CARMELITA

Ay, jai, jai. You want me to…? (*beat, acquiesces*) Good pilgrim, you do wrong your hand too much, which mannerly devotion shows in this: (*thinks for a moment to recall lines*) for saints have hands that pilgrims' hands do touch, and palm to palm is holy palmers' kiss.

FLUFFY

Have not saints lips, and holy palmers too?

CARMELITA

Ay, pilgrim, lips that they must use in prayer.

FLUFFY

O then, dear saint, let lips do what hands do; they pray – grant thou, lest faith turn to despair.

CARMELITA

Saints do not move, though grant for prayers' sake.

FLUFFY

Then move not while my prayer's effect I take (*kisses her*).
Thus from my lips, by thine, my sin is purged.

CARMELITA

Then have my lips the sin that they have took.

FLUFFY

Sin from my lips? O trespass sweetly urged! Give me my sin
again (*kisses her again*).

CARMELITA

You kiss by the book. (*beat, or two*) That's when the nurse
comes in.

FLUFFY

I know.

CARMELITA

You know, that is a sonnet.

FLUFFY

A what?

CARMELITA

A sonnet. Those lines Romeo and Juliet speak form a sonnet.

FLUFFY

(*dizzy with love for* CARMELITA) Uh – huh.

CARMELITA

Romeo and Juliet share a sonnet and within that sonnet they fall in love. And it's all inspired by Juliet. So, you see. A woman. (*she kisses him*) Beauty. (*she kisses him*)

FLUFFY

Class. (*kiss*)

CARMELITA

Elegance. (*kiss*)

FLUFFY

And inspires love. (*goes to kiss her but stumbles since she is not in front of him anymore*)

CARMELITA

So, now you see how you can fall in love if you meet the right cat. That was good practice, Mister eh-Fluffy.

FLUFFY

If I meet the right...?

CARMELITA

Jah, practice, for when you try and run out and get away; if you meet the right cat, you can do it!

FLUFFY

That...was practice?

CARMELITA

That was practice, sí.

FLUFFY

Oh.

CARMELITA

What did you think it was?

FLUFFY

I thought it was...*not* practice.

CARMELITA

Oh, come now, chico. For it not to be practice, your
intentions would have to be honorable; and I don't think –

FLUFFY

But they are! Honorable. Seriously.

CARMELITA

Come on. You don't have a ring or anything.

FLUFFY

I have this (*gives* CARMELITA *his collar*).

CARMELITA

Your collar?

FLUFFY

Carmelita. (*goes down on one knee*) Will you marry me.

CARMELITA

Marry you?

FLUFFY

Marry me.

CARMELITA

This is so sudden, no?

FLUFFY

Marry me. For better or for worse.

CARMELITA

For better or for worse?

138

FLUFFY

For better or for worse.

CARMELITA

I don't know about "worse," chico.

FLUFFY

Come on, that's the way it is. For better or for worse.

CARMELITA

OK. For better or for worse. Meow. And on the condition that you are always a good boy.

FLUFFY

And on the condition that I am always a good boy.

CARMELITA

And don't eat no bugs.

FLUFFY

And I won't eat no bugs (*they laugh*). And you'll be a good girl?

CARMELITA

Woman.

FLUFFY

You'll always be a good woman?

CARMELITA

Mira, I am always good.

FLUFFY

Yes, you are. So, marry me.

### CARMELITA

Um. Es posible. [It's possible.] Pero… [But] You can't be joking with me.

### FLUFFY

Not joking. Not joking at all. Look, cats' lives are shorter than peoples' lives, so we gotta make the most of what we have. Carmelita, I am here. On the floor. On one knee. Will you marry me?

### CARMELITA

O, señor eh-Fluffy! (*to audience, light shift*) What would my mother say?

### FLUFFY

Wait. What are you doing?

### CARMELITA

Women can be taken advantage of.

### FLUFFY

Are you talking to the audience?

### CARMELITA

She would probably say it's better to be married than not.

### FLUFFY

Hey, this is my play!

### CARMELITA

What would my father say?

### FLUFFY

Only I can talk directly to the audience!

### CARMELITA

What am I thinking, I don't even know who my father is.

FLUFFY

My play, do you hear? It's called 'Fluffy' not 'Carmelita'!

CARMELITA

(*to* FLUFFY) Ay, callate la boca y déjame en paz! [Shut your mouth and leave me alone!]Would you relax? I'm having a moment here!

FLUFFY

Oh, OK. Sorry. Go right ahead.

CARMELITA

(*to audience*) This is all so…surreal! So…bizarre. So…loco.

FLUFFY

Do you think you could come back to the world of <u>my</u> play now, please?

CARMELITA

(*to* FLUFFY) Oh, Mister eh-Fluffy! Sí! I will marry you!

FLUFFY

Oh, Carmelita! (*kisses her, then, to audience*) Sorry about that confusion, folks. (*to* CARMELITA) You have made me the happiest cat in the world!

CARMELITA

Me también! (*kisses him*) Oh, Mister eh-Fluffy! I hope you don't get tired of me.

FLUFFY

How could I? I adore you! Look, I'll keep you happy, and fed, and clean and get the spots you can't reach.

CARMELITA
Easy there, muchacho. Grooming is important, but you gotta
let me take care of myself as I see fit.

FLUFFY
Aw.

CARMELITA
I'll let you know when I need help.

FLUFFY
You will?

CARMELITA
I will.

FLUFFY
Let's do it now.

CARMELITA
Meeeroooww?!

FLUFFY
Let's get married now!

CARMELITA
Oh, sí. OK, bueno! (*they kiss*) Oh, Mister eh-Fluffy!

FLUFFY
Oh, Carmelita! (*another kiss*) Excuse me, one moment,
future Mrs. eh-Fluffy. I'm just going to visit the, uh, box.

CARMELITA
Of course, mi amor (*a quick kiss and* FLUFFY *exits*).
Marriage. What am I doing?

FLUFFY

(*offstage*) You talking to the audience again?

CARMELITA

No, just…just thinking out loud! (*to audience*) This is all like a dream – or a nightmare! I'm too young! And him? Do I really want to be señora Carmelita eh-Fluffy? I need a better last name. Like Banderas, o De León, o Iglesias! Well, maybe not Iglesias, but not eh-Fluffy, either! Who came up with the idea that the woman should take the man's last name? Do you know? No? You? I don't know either, but it wasn't a woman! Why do women have to even contemplate marriage? I mean, imagine a world without men. It'd be a world of fat, happy women! And look at him. And look at me. I'm beautiful! And he's…OK. (*vaguely to someone in audience*) You married beneath you, didn't you? I think all women do. Yes, I can see. You take care of yourself and he...? Well… My girlfriend who got married says that when a woman marries, she exchanges the attentions of many men for the <u>inattention</u> of one. But he is cute. And he is good to me. And I can see it when he looks at me. He does adore me. And he makes me laugh. I suppose, really, that is all one can hope for.

FLUFFY

(*entering*) Everything OK?

CARMELITA

O, sí, sí. (*beat, then, with resolve*) Sí. Todo está bien.

FLUFFY

OK. I'll get things around here set. (*runs into bathroom, gets a roll of toilet paper, comes back out*)

CARMELITA

I'll get myself ready (*goes into bedroom*).

FLUFFY

(*to the audience*) I'm so nervous. You ever get like this? I mean, my tummy is fluttering, my palms are sweating, I just went to the bathroom but I think I gotta pee again! I mean, I'm gonna be…married! This is all like a dream – or a nightmare!


CARMELITA

(*offstage*) And who are you talking to in there?


FLUFFY

Uh, I'm just thinking out loud, like you! Better make some preparations. (FLUFFY *creates a walkway with the toilet paper that leads from the bathroom/bedroom area, to center stage and then up and onto the coffee table. Depending on technical abilities of the space, the director may choose to have* FLUFFY *add other elements/decorations to create the right mood.*) When you begin to think of it, and it's not done yet, you begin to wonder if marriage is the right thing. It does seem easier to stay out than get out. I mean, do I really want to wake up next to the same person every morning? For the rest of my life? I just met her. But I don't think a person should know too precisely who he's marrying. Because then, there's nothing else to discover. And everything is great right now, but don't all married couples get to the point of 'she doesn't want to anymore and he can't anyway'? (*beat*) Doesn't matter. She is beautiful. Then again, they say beauty is only skin deep. Well, I've got no problem with skin-deep beauty; I mean, who cares about a beautiful small intestine? Ah, Carmelita. She's a fireball. She would add spice to life. She takes care of herself. She takes care of me. And she makes me want to be a better cat. (*beat*) I ain't gonna lie, how much better could I get? But, should I get married? (CARMELITA *enters wearing a sexy white dress.*) Yes. I should.


*In similar fashion to* PEPE'S *earlier song,*

DELILAH *and* NANCY *stand on the back platform. Schubert's "Ave Maria" begins (use a track or accompanist). Lights shift as in a surreal dream.*

CARMELITA *walks toward* FLUFFY. FLUFFY *gives* CARMELITA *flowers from the vase, she takes his hand, they both step up and onto the coffee table, and face the audience as* DELILAH *and* NANCY *underscore the marriage by singing Schubert's "Ave Maria" while* PEPE *officiates (see appendix for music).*

PEPE

Dearly beloved, we are gathered here today, with these witnesses including the audience who we don't really know except for those who we specially invited to come see this show,

FLUFFY

Hey, the only person who can talk directly to the audience is me.

PEPE

That's not true at all. We are here to celebrate the union entre these two gatos, señorita Carmelita and Mister eh-Fluffy. Ya lo se que es un poco loco [I know that it's a little crazy], pero they love each other, and they are gonna get married. Now, sabes that this is not to be entered lightly, but reverently, lovingly, solemnly, but also passionately and with good food and wine and a lot of dancing, cariños! Maybe salsa o flamenco, lo que quieras. Into this holy bond of matrimony, come these two frisky felines who have made this blessed decisión. If any person can show just cause why they may not be joined together, let them speak now or forever hold their peace (*looks out into audience*). Everyone seems to be pretty quiet so I'm gonna take that as a 'OK.' Please, you gonna repeat after me. Mister eh-Fluffy, you gonna go first. Ready?

FLUFFY

Ready.

PEPE

OK, I, Mister eh-Fluffy,

FLUFFY

I, Fluffy. There is no 'mister,' y'all.

PEPE

Take you, Carmelita.

FLUFFY

Take you, Carmelita.

PEPE

To be my wife, my friend, my faithful partner and my love from this day forward.

FLUFFY

To be my wife, my friend, my faithful partner and my love from this day forward.

PEPE

And to cherish you for as long as we both shall live.

FLUFFY

And to cherish you for as long as we both shall live.

PEPE

Bueno. Now you, Carmelita. I, Carmelita.

## CARMELITA

I, Carmelita.

## PEPE

Take you, Mister eh-Fluffy.

## CARMELITA

Take you, Mister eh-Fluffy.

## PEPE

To be my husband, my friend, my faithful partner and my love from this day forward.

## CARMELITA

To be my husband, my friend, my faithful partner and my love from this day forward.

## PEPE

And to cherish you for as long as we both shall live.

## CARMELITA

And to cherish you for as long as we both shall live.

## PEPE

Ah, sí! Bueno! By the power vested in me, by the state of [*wherever the play is being performed*], I now pronounce you husband and wife. Ya puede besar.

> *As* FLUFFY *and* CARMELITA *kiss, Jean Joseph Mouret's "Rondeau" or similar piece begins to play.* FLUFFY *scoops up* CARMELITA *and they exit, perhaps through the audience, as lights fade. Music might transition to something contemporary and upbeat.*

## Scene 2

*Same apartment. One year later.* FLUFFY *is asleep on the couch. He stretches a few times then, in a sudden burst, is awake. He looks around. All is well.*

FLUFFY

Well, hello! (*beat*) Again. And welcome to the almost-the-end-of-the-play. A coda, if you will. Now, I trust you all have enjoyed yourselves this evening [afternoon]. And I'd like to apologize for my earlier, uh, (*referring to the vomiting*) incident with the fly that I ate and, uh, well, what came up. These things happen. I'm sure that none of you good folks out there have ever had to deal with that sort of thing. (*not directly to anyone, but with focus into the audience*) Oh, wait. You have? Well, I'm sorry to hear that. Would you like to come up here and tell us about it? No? I thought not. That's why I'm apologizing for my incident. You'll also be happy to know that I've sworn off bugs. That's right. It's been a year to this day since I ate a bug and my resolve is just as strong to…not. (*this is hard*) Do it. Anymore. You could say that I have certain incentives in place. I have a beautiful wife – who would probably kill me if I did…and my pet, Delilah, would probably throw me out; and I've got five – count'em – five beautiful kittens!

CARMELITA

(*from offstage*) Oye, señor eh-Fluffy! Venga! Necessito ayuda con tus hijos! [Hey, Mr. Fluffy! Come! I need help with your children!]

FLUFFY

I'll be right there, my little habanero pepper! As you can see, we've got our paws full! And speaking of one-year benchmarks, today is our anniversary. And, yes, I do have an anniversary gift all picked out. Even sprinkled a little cat nip

FLUFFY (CONT)

on it, to give it that extra touch. I'll show you what it is in just a minute. Now, you might be wondering what happened with the other folks that appeared up here onstage with me tonight. (*As he speaks,* DELILAH *enters, finds a suitable position onstage to begin creating a final stage picture.*) Well, Delilah is doing just fine on her own. She gets a lot of writing done, speaks at community events, and advocates for the rights of others. (PEPE *enters, finds a suitable position onstage*) Pepe? He is still searching for Mr. Right. But while he does so, he lends a helping hand to Delilah – and to me and Carmelita! Oh, and Nancy (NANCY *enters, finds a suitable position onstage*). Nancy has actually begun growing. Yes, growing! A little. And I don't mean in terms of height. (*whispers*) Or weight. She has one of those Rosetta language learning programs so she can speak Spanish. She's even begun trying that mind-body wellness regime called 'yoga.' I've seen her do it. It's not pretty.

CARMELITA

Oye! Mister eh-Fluffy! Dónde estás, hombre?

FLUFFY

OK, OK! I'm coming! (*to audience*) Excuse me a minute (*Exits. Quickly returns holding four kittens – two in each of his hands, by the scruff of their necks; small stuffed animals should be used.* CARMELITA *also enters holding one kitten in her mouth.*) Don't worry y'all. They're not getting hurt. We're professionals. (*He gives two to* DELILAH, *and one each to* NANCY *and* PEPE). But the most important thing about all this is that we have these little additions that make up one big family. (*talking to the kittens*) Oh, my babies. There's so much I want to tell you. So much I want to impress upon you. Sisyphus, Camus, and happiness. I know I'll worry. I know I'll fret. But I will spend every moment caring for you and your well-being. But for now, a quick cleaning will have to do (*gives each kitten a quick lick arriving at* CARMELITA *last. He gazes at her lovingly for a moment. Next,* DELILAH *takes the kitten from* CARMELITA *as lights shift so that the focus is on* FLUFFY *and* CARMELITA, *downstage*).

CARMELITA

Mi amor.

FLUFFY

Carmelita. I have something for you.

CARMELITA

For me?

FLUFFY

(*Gets bag that has been strategically placed by couch*) Here.

CARMELITA

Should I open it now?

FLUFFY

Yes!

CARMELITA

(*opens bag, takes out a gray bean bag shaped like a rock, then, flatly*) What is this? A bean bag?

FLUFFY

(*very excited*) Shaped like a rock!

CARMELITA

(*flatly*) A bean bag shaped like a rock.

FLUFFY

Happy anniversary!

CARMELITA
Mister eh-Fluffy. Am I missing something?

FLUFFY
Don't you see? This is our rock – our miniature boulder that we can push around over and over again, for better or for worse, and always –

FLUFFY and CARMELITA
Be joyful!

CARMELITA
Oooohhh!

FLUFFY
Smell it. Go on, smell it!

CARMELITA
(*sniffs*) Ooof! Is that...?

FLUFFY
Not grass, but I did put some cat nip on it!

CARMELITA
(*immediately becomes frisky*) Oh, you know just what I like!

FLUFFY
And you know just what I like.

CARMELITA
(*warning*) Behave. (*lightens*) Oh, Mister eh-Fluffy.

FLUFFY
Mrs. eh-Fluffy.

CARMELITA
Meow.

FLUFFY

Meow. (*they kiss*)

*Fun, up-beat music as lights fade.*

<u>THE END</u>

# APPENDIX

*"Poesía" words and music by David Overton*

# Poesía

155